Climbing

Lene Gammelgaard was born in 1961 in L climbed some of the world's highest peaks and ha ocean sailor, a lawyer, a psychotherapist and a journalist. She co-founded several drug treatment centres in Copenhagen, where she now resides, and now works as a therapist and writer. *Climbing High*, a bestseller in Denmark, is Gammelgaard's first book. She is currently at work on her second.

Climbing High

A Woman's Account of Surviving the Everest Tragedy

Lene Gammelgaard

PAN BOOKS

First published in Denmark as *Everest: Vejen Til Toppen*
Copyright © 1996 by Lene Gammelgaard

First English edition published 1999 by Seal Press

This edition published 2000 by Pan Books
an imprint of Macmillan Publishers Ltd
25 Eccleston Place, London SW1W 9NF
Basingstoke and Oxford
Associated companies throughout the world
www.macmillan.co.uk

ISBN 0 330 39227 1

1 3 5 7 9 8 6 4 2

A CIP catalogue record for this book is available from
the British Library.

Printed and bound in Great Britain by
Mackays of Chatham plc, Chatham, Kent

For the children all over the world
who have lost a parent to the mountains

ACKNOWLEDGMENTS

My thanks to all who supported my participation on Sagarmatha Environmental Expedition 1996; to my brother Morten Gammelgaard for being my manager and my protector whenever the pressure grew too intense; and to my family and friends for their patience. Thanks also to Stig Andersen, my Danish editor, for daring, and to Ingrid Emerick, Faith Conlon and Jennie Goode of Seal Press for putting so much effort into giving *Climbing High* its true voice in another language.

CONTENTS

I had learned to take on the responsibility of great difficulties, and to remain true to myself at all times.

—Reinhold Messner, *Free Spirit*

FOREWORD

In the spring of 1996 I climbed Mount Everest, the highest mountain in the world, becoming the first Scandinavian woman ever to stand on top. I was a team member on the Sagarmatha Environmental Expedition, led by the internationally known and respected American mountaineer Scott Fischer.

What had been planned as the climb of a lifetime in the company of like-minded people—our charismatic guide, Scott, was legendary for gathering fun crews and guaranteeing high-spirited adventure—turned out instead to be clouded by tragedy.

The events that took place on Mount Everest on May 10 and 11, 1996, became news the world over. While climbers from Scott's team and from the team led by New Zealand guide Rob Hall were still on the summit or beginning their descent, a raging storm hit the mountain. Within forty-eight hours the death toll had reached an unprecedented number. Five people on the South Col route and three on the North Col route had perished in the storm, including my dear friend Scott. In all twelve lives were lost during the spring climbing season.

The press coverage was overwhelming. To those of us on the climb and to those who lost loved ones on the mountain, the scrutiny by the media was at times terribly intense. Over the following weeks and months, each team member tried to sort out his or her own experience of the tragedy, while the rest of the world was pressing for details—what exactly had happened up there? And, of course, there is no simple answer.

Since that fateful May climb, several books have been written about the Everest disaster, including this one, which was published in Denmark in the fall of 1996, becoming the first account to appear in book form. In early 1997, *Into Thin Air* by Jon Krakauer (a member of Rob Hall's Adventure Consultants Expedition) was published and became an overnight bestseller in the United States. Anatoli Boukreev, the world-famous guide who had helped lead Scott's team, wrote with his co-author, G. Weston DeWalt, his own account entitled *The Climb*, which was published in late 1997. Each book has provided a unique perspective on the diverse personalities of the Everest climbers and the chain of events that turned triumph into catastrophe, and each has given the public insight into the mix of magic and fear that accompanies the pursuit of the world's highest peak.

It seems that all mountaineers who continue to climb try to learn a lesson from the tragedies that take place, but the real lesson, ultimately, is that nature cannot be controlled. And for that lesson I am truly grateful. I summited Everest (the mountain known to Tibetans as *Chomolungma*, or Mother Goddess of the World) and was fortunate enough to survive to tell the tale. I have tremendous respect and—yes—love for this awesome mountain. I set out to test myself, and I was privileged that the greatest mountain in the world showed me my true size.

My attitude toward climbing now is the same as it was when I decided to risk the challenge of Everest: You must learn to take responsibility for yourself. The world's highest peaks are excellent teachers in this respect. In the so-called death zone above 26,000 feet, you just have to know and profoundly accept that "climbing high" is a survival game. It can be an extraordinary and deeply rewarding experience, but there is no escaping the fact that you can also die. Further, you cannot expect anybody to help you once you are up there. Your fate is in your own hands. Of course, there are unwritten codes of mountaineering conduct, and spectacular rescues do occur, but everything you do or do not do is ultimately your decision. You are responsible for yourself.

And isn't that ultimately the lesson of life anywhere?

O

I have always been a seeking soul, driven by some uncontrollable urge to challenge the parameters of my small world. As a young girl I drove my parents crazy—questioning norms, social conformity, gender roles, destiny itself. As I grew to adulthood, I suffered a lot of resistance because of my way of being, doubtless compounded by the fact that I was a woman. There were many times when I was told I couldn't, or shouldn't, do something because I was a woman. I did it anyway. I've never felt I had a choice—it is just who I am.

For twenty years or more I have written in black notebooks about the world around me. Painting pictures of reality with words as my instrument has always formed the core of my being. I am a writer. So when I decided to climb Everest, I wrote. I wrote before I left Denmark, I wrote at Base Camp, I wrote on the mountain and I wrote after the tragedy had unfolded in all its enormity.

In the immediate aftermath of the climb, I desperately needed time alone to deal with what had happened. On the way back to Denmark from the Himalaya, I stopped at a remote island in Thailand and stayed there for two weeks in complete isolation, trying to come to terms with the fact that my ultimate athletic challenge and grand adventure had transmuted into a devastating tragedy. I felt both extremely vulnerable and emotionally frozen. When I tried to write, the only sentence I could form was:

Scott is dead.

That is all I could express until I began working on this book.

When I returned to Denmark, my Danish publisher, Stig Andersen, tried to help me get going on the book project with various words of advice. Unable to respond, I finally told him that he needed to trust my inner creative process, to have faith and leave me in peace for a while. I knew the book was already written inside of me: "The book is finished; I can feel it—it just needs typing."

I spent the late summer of 1996 at a writing retreat. There I typed from early morning to late at night. In seclusion I was finally able to feel the soundless screams emerge from deep within. Screams of grief, of anger. And a feeling of desperation—a hunger—for life, after so much ice and death.

It was a painful process, one that forced me to strip away my defenses and confront what had happened. Scott was dead, yet there I sat, day after day, bringing him back to life with my words. I could hear his voice and see his grin. But the act of writing was a way for me to process my grief and slowly rediscover the gift of my mountain experiences—the pure joy of wilderness.

In this book I have tried to act as a camera lens, recording what I experienced, presenting my teammates as I saw them. Each reader will naturally form his or her own opinion, and I accept that as a writer and climber I cannot be completely objective. No person can be—especially when oxygen-deprived at extreme altitude.

What I want to share is not the death and tragedy of climbing, but the majestic beauty of the high mountains and the incredible experience of pursuing the challenge of Everest. The intense inner drive and personal discipline required to take on this mountain is a part of the experience, but so is the connection with other climbers, who are never perfect but are fantastic people to be with nonetheless. I want to share my love for the mountains, for the wilderness where I feel at home.

When I come back from a climb I feel renewed—a better human be-ing, stronger and more capable of living on life's unpredictable terms and conditions.

Today, I am grateful for the invaluable lessons I have learned from the mountains and for all of the adventures I shared with my team mem-bers—with Scott, with Anatoli, who died tragically in 1997, and with Lopsang Jangbu Sherpa, who was tragically killed by an avalanche on Everest a few months after our climb. Grateful for the new dimen-sions these people added to my existence. And less and less angry with them for no longer being here to play with me, to challenge me, to show me new routes in the mountains and in my life. I am still lonely for their company, I still cry. But today I try to carry on what they did so well—create adventures for others. Writing *Climbing High* was one way to do that.

In the first months following the book's release in Denmark I felt ter-ribly vulnerable. The story is about real people, and, therefore, what I wrote had real consequences. I worried about my ability to paint a true picture of the experience, to kill some of the myths connected with mountaineering that tend to distort the facts, without exposing my fellow climbers—and myself—to harsh examination by those who were not there. In the end, though, the book is my account, and my account alone.

The public response to *Climbing High* in Denmark has been over-whelmingly positive, and I am deeply grateful to the many people who have taken the time and effort to call, to stop me on the streets and to write me about the inspiration they received from the book. I have been told that I am a role model for young girls who want to pursue dreams less conventional than what might be expected of them—a responsibility I do not take lightly.

For my aim with *Climbing High* was not so much to write yet another mountaineering book. Of those there are plenty. Instead I hoped to be able to inspire people to take a closer look at their own lives, to consider whether they are living their dreams or postponing them. My belief is that life is meant to be lived fully, explored twenty-four hours a day. You can't wait till some other time to fulfill your innermost aspirations. You must pursue your goal and have the courage to persevere, even in the face of failure. The ability to learn from failure and grow through losses is a necessary part of any endeavor, no matter what your dream.

It is my hope that American readers will find inspiration in these pages. Perhaps my story will encourage you to expand your life in new ways, large or small. For if you never test your limits, how will you know what they are?

Lene Gammelgaard
Denmark
January 1999

Climbing
High

TEAM PARTICIPANTS

SAGARMATHA ENVIRONMENTAL EXPEDITION 1996

Expedition leader

Scott Fischer
Seattle, Washington

Martin Adams
Ketchum, Idaho

Neal Beidleman
Aspen, Colorado

Anatoli Boukreev
Almaty, Kazakhstan

Charlotte Fox
Aspen, Colorado

Lene Gammelgaard
Copenhagen, Denmark

Dale Kruse
Craig, Colorado

Tim Madsen
Aspen, Colorado

Sandy Hill Pittman
New York, New York

Klev Schoening
Seattle, Washington

Pete Schoening
Bothell, Washington

*Expedition doctor and
Base Camp manager*

Ingrid Hunt
New York, New York

Sherpa team members

Lopsang Jangbu Sherpa
climbing sirdar

Pemba Gyalzen Sherpa
climbing Sherpa

Ngawang Tendi Sherpa
climbing Sherpa

Ngawang Topche Sherpa
climbing Sherpa

Tashi Tschring Sherpa
climbing Sherpa

Tendi Sherpa
climbing Sherpa

Ngawang Dorje Sherpa
climbing Sherpa

Ngawang Sya Kya Sherpa
climbing Sherpa

Gyalzen Sherpa
Camp II cook

Ngima Kale Sherpa
Base Camp sirdar

Mingma Sherpa
Base Camp cook

Krishna Rahadur Rai
kitchen staff

Pemba Sherpa
kitchen staff

Kajee Sherpa
mail runner

PROLOGUE

SUMMER 1991, NEPAL

The unspoiled, the unknown was what I sought when the gypsy and the adventurer in me needed to break out of the limitations of ordinary living. The Aborigines of Australia call it "walkabout"—leaving their work to go wandering in the bush for months, in harmony with nature, then returning and simply continuing with life as if they had never been away.

After three months of exploring and testing myself in Nepal, at higher altitudes than Europe could offer, it was now time for me to go home—to put the risky, the adventurous behind me, to grow up, become mature. To learn how to live peacefully and find serenity and contentment in the everyday life that dominates most people's existence.

I suppose I was slightly relieved by the realization that the high mountains were inhabited by crazy people, people who didn't seem to be capable of finding satisfaction in life. On the other hand, I was also a bit disappointed about my own ordinariness—that I, apparently, didn't have that kind of "drive." But these sentiments I admitted only to myself.

I knew deep within that it was utterly foolish to try to reach the summit of the world at the risk of my life. I did not believe that happiness lay at the top of the world's highest mountain. Nor did I believe that—once having stood on top—I, or life, would change or become better.

"You will be back to climb Everest," an elderly mountaineer from the United Kingdom told me as I prepared to return to Denmark. I did not agree with his prophecy, but flattered by his perception of me, I said nothing.

APRIL 9, 1996, EVEREST BASE CAMP

"Wouldn't it be great if we could have this expedition over and done with, without any injuries or major accidents?" Scott asks over a mug of Starbucks coffee.

I don't answer. We both know that what happens, happens.

But it's good to be back. Good to be back in Nepal. To be back in the region of the Sherpas. Here I feel at home. Today, sitting in Base Camp—recollecting, contemplating the web of experiences that has brought me back to Everest—I am happy.

Part I

The Point of No Return

The Invitation

SUMMER 1995

It's early morning on the Baltoro Glacier in Pakistan. Scott and I are headed for Concordia, a giant crossroads created by some of the largest glaciers in the Himalayan mountains. I have just spent a month in Pakistan, trekking in to Broad Peak Base Camp in the Karakoram Range. Broad Peak (26,402 feet/8,047 meters), neighbor to the notorious mountain K2, is Scott's next expedition. I'm on my way out of Base Camp to meet up with my team to climb the steep Gondogoro La Pass. Scott insists on joining me on the two-hour hike.

Enormous massifs surround us: Gasherbrum II, III and IV, Mitre Peak, Chogolisa, Broad Peak and, behind us, the characteristic pyramid shape of K2. Here on the glacier, just before our roads part, Scott asks the question that will change my life.

"Do you want to climb Everest with me in spring 1996?"

It takes only a second from the moment the message hits the receptors of my brain to formulate my answer.

"Yes!"

No spontaneous doubt. Nothing. Just inner certainty. I know Scott is serious about his invitation. And he knows I am serious in my commitment. My words and actions correspond.

Now he just has to survive his Broad Peak expedition.

What just happened—his question, my response—makes me think of something I wrote in my journal . . .

It is possible for us to celebrate life and transform the invisible into the visible. To experience that our existence is a whole. This is how life can be perceived by the creative human being. Because when we reach the point where we stop trying to control reality, we become capable of accepting, welcoming, what is offered us.

Freedom for me is learning to accept reality—with all its contradictions and paradoxes, the formidable and discouraging aspects as well as the pure and inspiring. The freedom of limitation.

Therefore, it is possible for me—with no doubt whatsoever—to want Everest 100 percent. My *yes* is a tribute to the subtlety of life. A return to innocence, leaving the defeats and sorrow of the past behind. It is a *yes* to trusting my own strength to carry this project through successfully. It is a *yes* to life's grandeur. It is a *yes* to trusting that there might be a meaning to my life. A *yes* to a naiveté that does not correspond with my life experiences and cynicism, but is rather the pureness that might follow the total resignation of a human being.

For several years I've been working with drug addicts, spending my life's energy on the dark side of existence, and now I'm in need of input from people who have succeeded in life. People who set fun goals and achieve them. People who don't take themselves too seriously because their outlooks are characterized by victories. Climbing the highest mountain in the world with a kindred spirit tempts me to return to the light. It is a *yes* that opens the floodgates at my core. All blocked energy is now coursing freely—wanting Mount Everest!

And why shouldn't I climb the highest mountain in the world?

I know that this drive is more than the desire to summit Everest, much more than the rather superficial act of climbing to the top of that mountain. For periods of my life I have hidden from the world because that was what I needed to do. But it's obvious that now I must grow, I must strive to reach my full potential—in spite of my desire to escape the responsibility that follows. Maybe now I am ready to bear the responsibility of living a significant life with a wider horizon.

O

August 13, 1995

Dear Lene,

Greetings from Islamabad.

I am grateful to inform you that Scott Fischer and two clients summited Broad Peak this morning at 9:05. More are headed for the summit. We wish them all good luck and a safe trip down and send our best regards to you.

I regret that we were not able to meet when you returned from Chitral, but some urgent business came up. Hope everything is well—talk to you later. Hope to meet up with you next time you are in Pakistan.

All the best,
Abdul Quddus
General Manager
Nazir Sabir Expeditions

Later that day I received an update from Scott himself on my answering machine: "I reached the summit and am safe down in Base Camp. Do you still want to climb that big thing with me?"

Finally it is time to work toward Everest: to intensify my climbing training and get sponsors to cover my share of the expenses.

Not long after Scott's telephone message, a letter arrives:

Broad Peak Base Camp
August 16, 1995

Dear Lene,

Thanks so much for your letters. The crisis right now is seven dead on K2. On the 13th we all summited Broad Peak, and Mountain Madness did good. Late afternoon a hellacious wind came up (we were already down to Camp III). It killed those still on K2. They called from the summit at 6:00 P.M.—that's the last we ever heard from them . . .

My friends Rob Slater, Geoff Lakes and Alison Hargreaves all died. Plus three Spaniards and a guy from New Zealand. The only contact to the world outside is our illegal satellite phone . . . It makes me realize how frail we actually are. That we are playing a deadly game. I don't want to be dead—I want to be alive . . .

Did you get my message on your machine? I do hope so.

This is all pretty painful. Alison leaves two kids. Same ages as mine. (A lot of tears.) Major bummer. Don't let me die, Lene. Keep me humble. (I am probably not humble, but I need to be.) The mountains are supreme. Most powerful. You should have seen it, Lene, the wind came up and just killed them. Geoff Lakes turned around and found his way back down to Camp IV, but he got killed by an avalanche that hit the tent during the night. Bivvier came as far down as Camp III, just to find it destroyed. He forced himself to crawl down to Camp II, where his friends were, but died during the night. None of the remaining managed to climb down. We can see a corpse on the slopes. It's a major tragedy.

Alison was the driving force toward the summit, with little respect for the power of K2. K2 won. What strikes me just now is that I trust my survival skills totally. But I had the same trust in their ability to survive—those who are now dead—and they had similar confidence in themselves. And they died. I must be careful . . .

The expedition blues are here. I'll start hiking . . .

Scott

O

To grow up is to learn that one's mature life consists of a sum of personal choices and decisions, and to realize that options give freedom. To dare to take upon oneself the responsibility and the pain in this kind of freedom is the condition of living.

My life and the time span that makes up my life are my concern. It is up to me and me alone to decide how I will spend my life—and the consequences of each choice are my responsibility.

The Preparations

One day I receive a letter from Scott with a short plan for the trek and the climbing schedule for Mount Everest:

> *Our goal is to get as many climbers as we can as safely as possible to the summit. To summit the highest mountain in the world will stretch the limits of our physiques and psyches to the utmost. To reach the top of Mount Everest is one of the greatest athletic challenges in the world. Correct training will be crucial so that we arrive well prepared for this extreme challenge.*
>
> *On Everest, attitude and mental toughness will determine who reaches the summit.*

PROGRAM

March 23, 1996   Departure on Thai Air for Kathmandu, Nepal.

March 24–27   Climbing team arrives. We will meet at Hotel Manang in the Thamel district of

Kathmandu. Our local agent, P.B. Thapa, will take care of the last details. The expedition members meet our high-altitude Sherpas. Lopsang Jangbu Sherpa is the sirdar, leader of the climbing Sherpas.

March 28–30   Helicopter to Lukla (9,200 ft/2,800 m). We rest three days in Namche to acclimatize. Team up with our Base Camp crew and porters. Control luggage and gear.

March 31   *To arrive on foot to the home of the Sherpas is like gaining insight into how it must have been for the Jews to arrive in the Holy Land.*
     — Mike Thompson, anthropologist and mountaineer

We start trekking toward Everest Base Camp. In about a week's time we'll have to gain 2,000 meters (6,560 feet) of altitude from Namche. First day, we'll traverse the mountainside along the Dudh Kosi valley, cross the river and ascend through pine, fir and rhododendron forest, to Tengboche (12,700 ft/3,870 m), where we'll camp next to Tengboche Monastery.

April 1   From Tengboche we cross the river Imja Khola, trekking up to Pheriche (14,000 ft/4,270 m) and the Himalayan Rescue Association's Trekkers Aid Post.

April 2   Resting day in Pheriche. An easy trip to Dingboche to improve acclimatization. Great

views of Ama Dablam and the Nuptse-
Lhotse Face.

April 3   From Pheriche the trail climbs steeply to the
                     end moraine of the Khumbu Glacier and fol-
                     lows it to Lobuche (16,170 ft/4,930 m). From
                     Lobuche we see Everest's South Wall and
                     most of the West Ridge route.

April 4   We proceed to the two shepherds' shelters in
                     Gorak Shep (16,958 ft/5,170 m) and establish
                     camp at the base of Kala Pattar. Views of
                     Pumori, Nuptse and Everest. Our route fol-
                     lows the Khumbu Glacier, on the moraine as
                     on the glacier itself.

April 5   Early rise to scramble up Kala Pattar (18,443
                     ft/5,554 m). From the top are the best photo
                     options of Mount Everest. We descend this
                     famous outlook and make our way to Everest
                     Base Camp, following yak trails through the
                     labyrinth of the Khumbu Glacier.

April 6–26   We arrive at Everest Base Camp (17,600 ft/
                     5,364 m) and make ourselves at home on the
                     glacier under the notorious Khumbu Icefall,
                     taking sufficient time to acclimatize. We climb
                     the Icefall, establish Camps I and II in the
                     Western Cwm, climb the Lhotse Face and
                     establish camp at the exposed Camp III. Sleep
                     a couple of nights in Camp III (24,000 ft/
                     7,315 m) to maximize acclimatization.

| April 27–30 | With the entire team in super condition, we return to Base Camp. Rest will be our main priority. Trekkers support team visits. We eat, rest and make final preparations for the summit bid. |

| May 1–4 | Ready for the summit bid, we climb directly to Camp II. Rest day. Camps III and IV. Those who are fit climb to Camp IV in South Col (26,000 ft/7,925 m). Going for the summit. |

| May 5–7 | We climb in the footsteps of the legends of climbing history. The ultimate goal of mountaineering transforms into reality. We summit Mount Everest (29,028 ft/8,848 m)! |

| May 8 | After descending from the summit, we return to Base Camp and prepare for the trek out. |

| May 15–20 | We fly out of Syangboche by helicopter when our yaks arrive with the expedition gear. |

| May 17–20 | Stay at high-class Hotel Yak & Yeti. Party! And good-bye. |

At first I feel elated reading through the expedition plan because it makes reaching the top of the world sound so easy, as if anybody can achieve it. Just follow the schedule, step by step, and you reach the goal. No problem.

Our itinerary makes me forget reality—for a little while. Maybe it *is* that easy. Maybe they are right, the people who claim that anybody can climb Everest. But most of those people haven't even set foot in the Himalaya! And if it is that easy, where's the ultimate challenge? Then again, my chances for success are bigger, and that prospect appeals to my laziness.

"If climbing Everest is as easy as you make it sound in this plan, I'm not even sure I want to climb that mountain," I tell Scott on the phone. We have a tacit agreement that he calls once a week—that is, if he is not traveling, on an expedition or slide show tour, or doing a photo session, commercial or the like. We are trying to coordinate "the business Lene Gammelgaard" with the introduction of his company, Mountain Madness, to the European market.* Simultaneously we do the best we can to make Everest happen.

I draw on Scott's experience with high-altitude climbing: What equipment shall I use? Which ice axes do you take? How do I prepare myself to climb the highest mountain on this planet without supplemental oxygen? Scott has been there, has done it, so I take his recommendations seriously.

Scott is a man of vision and has proven, by the way he lives his life, that he makes dreams become real. But sometimes his wishful thinking stretches the bounds of reality. Or I guess it's more correct to say that what he plans is possible, but typically requires more time than he prophesies. That's where I play my role, patience learned through disappointments. If you have patience and endurance, almost anything is possible.

Scott and I met in Nepal in 1991. We have corresponded over the years and, through writing, have gotten to know each other. I see Scott the human being more than I see Scott the "American hero—one of the

*Scott and I had discussed my joining his team and representing Mountain Madness in Denmark as a way to open up the European market. My Everest ascent would help generate publicity in Europe for me and and for Mountain Madness.

world's strongest climbers." He comes from another culture, is used to strong, competent women in the high mountains, and thinks it's natural that I can "climb that big thing."

I realize that I actually thrive on being believed in, being backed up—something Americans are good at, and something that I, being Danish, had looked down on as a superficial and pathetic phenomenon. But it does help me!

Actually, it ought to be me—the less experienced climber—who believes it's easy and Scott who punctures my illusions, but it is the other way around. My experience in the mountains can't convince me that it's simple—on the contrary. My experience is that nature determines.

After all, how many winter seasons have I spent in the Chamonix Aiguilles, with great plans and aspirations to climb this and that route, and, winter after winter, been rejected by the weather? Gale, snow, whiteout and various cocktails of weather have left many an ambition unfulfilled.

To me it's the most natural fact in the world: Nature determines!

If you come from a small country like Denmark and therefore don't live with the breadth of nature's catastrophes—other than as thrilling entertainment on TV—it can be a shock to learn that, in other parts of the world, nature is the master of what you can and cannot do, that nature can be deadly in all its greatness.

I do not believe I can *conquer* Mount Everest, but I do hope I will be capable of estimating the conditions and be allowed to ascend Chomolungma, "Mother Goddess of the Earth," with due respect and humility in the face of her powers.

I am frightfully aware that if nature rises in all its might, I stand no chance. And no fine plan will make any difference then. That is what I discuss with Scott this morning.

"What about the weather, Scott? What if it doesn't adapt to your schedule? I also find it hard to see that the itinerary gives me sufficient time for acclimatizing properly to climb without oxygen. Your plan is made for the bulk of the expedition, who are climbing with oxygen."

"If you really want to climb without oxygen, I will back you," Scott answers.

The Everest trip is actually a double expedition: Everest as first priority and then Lhotse, the neighboring mountain and the fourth highest in the world. Moreover, Scott has his own ambitions and will, if time allows, make a summit attempt on Manaslu (26,781 ft) with other world-class climbers attempting Everest this season.

My ego wants to bag Lhotse as well as Everest in my first 8,000-meter season,* but common sense says otherwise, and my name is not on the climbing permit for Lhotse. I stick to one goal at a time; otherwise I would unconsciously begin dividing my mental energy between the two mountains and risk not gaining the summit of either.

I believe we see the world differently, Scott and I. I have had numerous setbacks in the mountains; Scott has had, for a period of five years, nothing but success on his expeditions. Except, that is, for Mount McKinley in 1995 when, profoundly astonished, he wrote to me, "I am back from Alaska. Guess what? Mount McKinley beat me this time.

---

*Fourteen mountain summits in the Himalaya and Karakoram are above 8,000 meters (26,240 feet), the so-called death zone, in which humans cannot survive for long because of extreme cold, severe weather and "thin" air. A world-class mountaineer might set a goal of summiting all the "8's" which Reinhold Messner accomplished in 1986.

It was the worst weather I have ever seen, anywhere."

His defeat by the weather made me smile and think, "So much the better if nature teaches you a bit of humbleness." I didn't think this out of malice, but because I care about Scott and wish him a long life. He has already survived longer than I dared believe when we first met in 1991.

Back then, I kept my distance from this big, boyish guy who climbed high mountains for the fun of it and partied like a madman. I had a feeling that one day I would receive the news that Scott Fischer had perished in the mountains. But it didn't happen. Instead, one letter followed another, recounting his climbs of peaks around the globe.

Maybe it's just me who's paranoid. Maybe it is possible to indulge in mountaineering and expeditions without getting killed. Maybe—just perhaps—you can't equate climbing with death. A few manage to pull through and create the grandest adventures as well as living a long life, including marriage, children and grandchildren. Maybe it is possible?

Our climbing itinerary fulfills my desire to make the chaos of life manageable. Scott makes the intangible secure by writing up a plan—black print on white paper—and thereby convinces others, as well as himself, that this is how reality has to be. We are in control.

But I know that some choose to trust our climbing itinerary to avoid taking complete responsibility for themselves. I want to trust that all is going to run smoothly—and why shouldn't it?

THE PERMIT
The phone's ringing jolts me from the realms of dreaming. I enjoy

sleeping and dreaming and have experienced how dreams can be a guide to finding my way in the infinity of being awake. I've learned to respect the potential information I can receive from more spiritual tribes than ours. And I detest being roused by something ringing. Alarms clocks are the worst. The fine balance of mind and matter gets disturbed. But this rousting at four on a November morning is less horrible than most because, before I grasp the receiver, I know it's Scott phoning from Kathmandu.

"I came across a good friend out here and invited him to climb Everest with us in the spring. It's Anatoli Boukreev, Russian superclimber. Have you seen the James Bond movie *Moonraker?* Anatoli is a lot like the guy with the metal jaws."

I interrupt: "Do you have it?"

Scott is in Kathmandu for a week—in his role as businessman and expedition leader—meeting with his dear friend and Nepali working partner, P.B. Thapa, and diverse "officials"—meetings at the Ministry of Tourism, meetings with the right people in the right ministries, all in the battle and race for a climbing permit for Everest via the South Col route during the spring 1996 climbing season.

"Do you have it—the permit for Everest?"

"Nah, not yet. But we'll get it!"

I know that Scott needs that certainty as much as I do—if not more. For years he's worked systematically toward making the Everest expedition the culmination of his business as a professional mountain guide. The success of his company depends on having that permit. Mountain Madness has arranged almost the entire expedition without knowing whether the promised permit will be issued.

I know Scott well enough to realize that his "But we'll get it!" expresses the belief he needs to have to make things happen—the same kind of belief I have to have to make summiting the highest mountain in the world a reality for me.

In each other's company, Scott and I achieve a knife-edge balance of enthusiasm, realism, criticism and mutual encouragement. We know that each of us has more than a full load to attend to, and we see each other through the momentary depressions which, for my part, stem from the hard work of fundraising.

We find a balance amid the psychic strain of knowing that what we are planning is a dangerous game. When stressed and excited it's tempting to complain and moan, but such behavior is useful only if somebody exists who can fix the world for you. We both recognize that those negative exclamations are sure death for the initiative that's necessary to overcome all—*all*—hindrances on the path toward the goal. We remind each other: *I am responsible for myself in this*.

The climbing permit is the all-important key to transforming the media show that I have sparked here in Denmark into reality on the mountain. *Lene Gammelgaard* written on that piece of paper will be permission to set my feet on the Khumbu Icefall in four months. A few letters worth $10,000. Oh! I so intensely hope that everything is fine, so that I won't make a public fool of myself and the sponsors that have committed themselves so far. I want to get to the top of Everest—and safely return!

The Training

I never talk or think about my ambition to summit Everest in terms of getting to the top at any price. Every time I mention it, think about it, train to achieve it, I say out loud or think to myself, "To the summit and safe return."

On the inside of the front door to my colorful little flat, I've pasted two pictures. One is a large photo of Hillary Step, the hardest technical climbing bit on our route up Everest—mixed climbing of vertical rock, ice and snow, just a short distance below the summit of the highest mountain in the world. On the photo I've printed in huge letters:

TO THE SUMMIT AND SAFE RETURN
Train harder.
Climb longer.

I am a believer in mental training. Years spent absorbed in psychological literature, education as a therapist and practical work with the human psyche have revealed to me that we humans are a bit like computers. Through our upbringing, culture and life experiences, we are programmed—and program ourselves—in certain ways. Being aware of this, one can indoctrinate oneself to a certain degree. At least that's the strategy behind my mental preparation for ascending Everest.

So I start the training, the indoctrination, with simply stated imperatives:
>>Train to climb by climbing.
>>Improve my mountaineering skills and knowledge of our route by reading expedition reports.
>>Talk to and learn from those who have been there.
>>Think of Mount Everest—to the summit and safe return—while climbing, swimming, jogging and practicing Tai Chi.

I prepare myself for each passage up the mountain from the route descriptions I have collected, prepare myself for the climb to the summit—prepare myself to win! I shut out—consciously—all doubts, all thoughts of death, frostbite and turning around because of bad storms.

And I make myself alarmingly goal-oriented, narrow-minded.

I consume the necessary literature on the medical hazards of high-altitude climbing—acute mountain sickness (AMS), pulmonary edema, cerebral edema—well enough to diagnose the symptoms, to know what to do under the circumstances, but choose not to go deeper. I shut my eyes to the health risks inevitably connected with oxygen deprivation on 8,000-meter peaks. Naturally it's not good for the brain or the body to function on too little oxygen for a sustained period of time, so I just don't think about that.

Selectively, I study the accounts of successful expeditions and communicate with people who have a playful, positive attitude toward mountaineering. My incentive is to code my mind with enough positive input to overrule my own healthy scepticism and to forget the stories I myself have gathered over the years as arguments against climbing mountains. I have made frequent use of them—with others as well as myself.

One story I heard as a young climber had an unforgettable impact on me. In 1985, I first heard rumors about the woman who sits at 27,600 feet on Mount Everest, her long blond hair blowing in the never-ending wind. The Norwegian mountaineer and expedition leader Arne Næss, Jr., describes his encounter with her:

> It's not far now. I can't escape the sinister guard. Approximately 100 meters above Camp IV she sits leaning against her pack, as if taking a short break. A woman with her eyes wide open and her hair waving in each gust of wind. It's the corpse of Hannelore Schmatz, the wife of the leader of a 1979 German expedition. She summited, but died descending. Yet it feels as if she follows me with her eyes as I pass by. Her presence reminds me that we are here on the conditions of the mountain.

The body of Hannelore Schmatz has since been removed. For that I am glad. Many mountaineers die on their way down from a successful summiting. And being a woman, I notice the destiny of my female kin. The British climber Julie Tullis died on K2 descending from the summit. She succumbed to exhaustion in her team's highest camp during a storm. And, of course, Scott's friend, Alison Hargreaves, a world-renowned mountaineer, died on K2, also after summiting.

I am planning my fundraising and training with the aim of being on board Thai Air on March 23 bound for Kathmandu. Nepal as intermediate goal is nothing compared with the stamina I will need to reach the actual summit. And the self-reliance necessary during these preparations is nothing compared to that demanded to survive the high mountains when it truly counts.

Best when it counts . . .

So, to me, it becomes impossible to complain about anything whatsoever in this everyday living because the vision of what awaits me puts any difficulty into perspective.

The second picture on my door is the painting of a clown—a multicolored, happy clown, created by my lovely niece Lise. The clown is there to remind me to have fun. After all, what achievement is worth anything if you are incapable of enjoying life while striving to get there? The process ought to be worth the goal, because even if you get to the summit, you can't remain there. I need the clown to draw my attention to enjoying what I'm arranging and to emphasize that even though climbing Mount Everest is serious business, it's only considered news for a short while. In a hundred years it's all forgotten.

Humans set goals for themselves throughout their lives. They achieve some and set new ones . . . so it's all about enjoying the journey of life while it lasts. And what is a goal anyway?

Select only the most sublime; force of habit will take care of the rest.

OBSESSION

I have chosen obsession. Or have I? What determines why we act in one way or another in our lives, or abstain from choosing?

I realize that, at any point, I can make a new choice. Any day, any time, I can decide whether I'm still willing to pay the price for the way to the summit. I realize that my choices—even choosing to bail out at this point—have consequences.

This time, I train to win, to get to the top of the world. In the past, I didn't think and act as I do now: I was more flexible, more compromising; I wanted to tread on an even path, and I guess I succeeded. What has this challenge sparked in me? Am I a gambler, who ticks only when this much is at stake? Or is it simply the right circumstances coming together at the right time?

Normally I try to find answers to questions like these. Analyze. Perhaps I have finally achieved the state of just living—living without pondering too much about it.

To the summit and safe return.

This self-programming will fuel my body in the thin air above 23,000 feet. I know that all motivation will disappear as I climb upward. Oxygen deprivation causes nausea and extreme headaches and debilitates the will and the ability to think straight, so every cell in my system must be charged with "To the summit and safe return." That will drive me up and back down, even when my brain tells me I am exhausted and can do no more.

The hazard of my little experiment is that by focusing entirely on the summit, victory becomes all-encompassing and may be so powerful a motive that I will be incapable of turning around before the summit, even at the cost of my health . . . or my life. Sometimes the true victory is to let go, to be capable of turning around in due time without suffering defeat. I have practiced this for five years. Have I mastered it?

The well-balanced person strives not only for a goal but lives fully in the flow of life, because every expression in the process is equally important:

> *What vanity in the art of Zen archery, wanting to hit the target!*
> *There will always be one stronger than you. The only importance is*
> *the correctness of the movement. — Kungfutse*

INSECURITY

Many people I've talked to about Everest have a certain idea of what an expedition is like, what it must be, to answer their perceptions of reality. Sometimes they even become insulted or offended if the facts I deliver do not correspond with their imaginings. Then I turn inward and become mute, sinking into the stored-up loneliness from other times I have expressed myself earnestly and found no understanding. It makes me insecure—for a little while—till I regain the inner strength, the faith, that I have the right to perceive the world and live in it the way I am.

A fax arrives from Mountain Madness—from Karen Dickinson, the company business manager. I've told her that I transferred the money to cover my portion of the climbing permit, porters and so on. She claims I haven't and, therefore, can't go with the expedition. "You are off the climbing permit. You cannot climb Mount Everest."

What a shock! Just when I trusted everything was finally falling into place.

Not climb Everest?

Never! No way!

No matter what, I will climb to the top of that mountain. (And safely return.)

Scott is already headed for Kathmandu, so he can't help me. My friends Flemming and Kirsten Marie keep me company in my small flat in the midst of the mess of expedition gear. Flemming believes it's possible to work everything out with Karen, but my patience with her mistrust is wearing thin. Why, I've already delivered two expedition duffel bags to Wilson Air Freight, the firm that has so generously sponsored the weight Thai Air doesn't cover.

Pretty difficult to keep cool just now, I am pissed and act with cold-blooded speed. I grab the phone and call sponsors and others who are part of this web. And the armies turn out. Documentation on long-ago transferred amounts is faxed across the Atlantic. Den Danske Bank traces the check that, according to arrangements, was sent ten days ago. Tears well up in my eyes—I'm moved by the support and fighting spirit from strangers who are helping this project become reality. Where have you been all my life? I am grateful for the experience and for the friends who are there, because I need them.

One thing I do know: I will be on board that plane tomorrow. And I will climb that mountain.

Part II

ॐ

The Arrival

Departure: Copenhagen

Copenhagen, March 23

THE FIRST DANISH WOMAN ON HER WAY
TO THE ROOF OF THE WORLD

It is not obvious that 34-year-old Lene Gammelgaard took her first step on the dangerous journey toward the stormy summit of Mount Everest this Saturday. Smiling and eagerly chatting, she checked in at Copenhagen Airport with 82 kilos of expedition gear. "And yesterday I shipped another 100 kilos," Gammelgaard puffs.

Gammelgaard will be—if all goes well—the first Scandinavian woman on the summit of the highest mountain in the world. The Danish mountaineer does not stress that she is a woman. "But it's a good story for the press and therefore interesting for my sponsors, who are financing this adventure," says Gammelgaard.

On May 8, she expects to set foot on the summit of Mount Everest, on the border of Nepal and Tibet, as a member of an American expedition. Apart from fulfilling the ambitions of the climbers, the expedition will play the role of garbageman and, in cooperation with local helpers, clean up the 8,848-meter-high mountain. Their predecessors have left tons of empty oxygen bottles, cans and tents in their attempts to climb the roof of the world, and the Sagarmatha Environmental Expedition 1996 wants to clean up the slopes. The nine climbing freaks are not adding to the piles of waste as they will clean up their camps.

Asked if she is scared of the hazardous mission, Gammelgaard replies: "I am no more frightened about this climb than I was sitting behind the wheel driving to the airport today—just imagine if anything had happened on the way!" She also entertains no illusions about becoming happier by summiting the mountain. "Maybe I'll wonder—What on earth am I doing here?—when I finally get there. But I can't help it. Adventure tempts, and I guess it will be great fun and intense cooperating with the group," says Gammelgaard, who's been climbing since 1985.

The next major project in her life will not be another mountain, but having a family. "I believe that will be at least as huge of a challenge. But hardly a story that the media and the sponsors will find interesting," she laughs. — LUI

Thai Air has upgraded me from coach to business class on the Copenhagen–Bangkok route. Love it when that happens. Whether the upgrading is due to Everest fame or just customary overbooking, I don't know.

I am sitting in the aisle seat. The window space is occupied by a gentleman in his forties. We do not communicate as we indulge in the customary glass of champagne exclusive globetrotters like us receive from the ever polite flight attendants as soon as our carry-on luggage is stowed over our heads.

At last I am on my way! Finally I can leave eight months of stress and pressure behind. At long last I can begin—again—to concentrate, focus on, what this circus is really all about: climbing the highest mountain in the world. And find the peace, the serenity, lost over the last two weeks when I put everything at stake to get out of Copenhagen.

Finally I can escape the business side of the expedition. Reunite with the genuine Lene, the true human being behind the machine I had to transform myself into to create contacts and mutually satisfying cooperation with the sponsors. I accepted and played by the rules that count in "society"—played a new role in a part of the world I long ago retreated from. And I have succeeded.

We amuse ourselves, my seatmate and I—two grownups, who for the next sixteen hours will share life in these seats. Even if we in business class have more space than those in the back, it's unavoidable that our elbows occasionally clash.

The printed menu arrives, distributed by the Thai crew. I love flying Thai Air. I find delight in the discreet, smiling attendants. Not too close—the same friendly distance that I sense in the population of Nepal, and which I now long for with my entire being.

I have become unaccustomed to living luxuriously, so I feel a little awkward being in business class again. I sense that everybody notices that it's been a long time since I was one of them. How is it that one is supposed to behave? My seatmate orders chicken for his main course.

"What's most Thai?" I ask the flight attendant.

"Chicken."

I fell head over heels in love with Thai cuisine back in 1988, when I was employed as chief buyer in the textile company Pinetta and the manager, Jens Jørgensen, and I were on business in Asia. Now I'm looking forward to eating it again.

Jens Jørgensen is part of this trip, too. His new company, First Concern, is one of my numerous sponsors. The name First Concern arose during a visit at the most expensive hotel in Singapore. All the hotel personnel wore small nameplates over their hearts, but instead of their names, the inscription read "You are my first concern." It took me a long time to grasp the full meaning of this message. But when Jens was in the process of finding a suitable name for his new business, I suggested the name First Concern. How pleased I am that his company has contributed the biggest logo flag for the summit, and it weighs less than a half-ounce!

In my hunt for money to finance the costs of this climb, I combined two ideas from previous expeditions: Stacy Allison, the first American woman to summit Everest, took flags to the summit as tokens for friends. Scott Fischer, on his successful 1994 Everest expedition, sold shares to people. By donating a certain amount of cash, they became part of the Everest support team and received newsletters as the expedition progressed. For a bigger handful of cash, they could "adopt" a transportation yak. Scott would then shoot a picture of "Maggie's yak," for example, and post it to her with the autographs of all the expedition members.

"The American Yakway" wouldn't go over so well with the Danes, but I picked up on the idea of people becoming a part of the project by contributing what I was in desperate need of—namely, cool cash. Late one night the inspiration came over me. By contributing a certain amount of money, a company could have its logo on the top of the world. I would personally carry it up there, take a photo—which would become the company's property—and then carry the flag down again (after all, I'm part of an environmental expedition). What a grand idea!

It took some explaining to uncomprehending and well-intentioned advertising people, however, when they delivered extravagant flags with halyards and everything, and I was forced to return it all: "Too huge, too heavy. No, I will not be able to take a flagpole to attach it to! Every gram of weight will mean the difference between failure and victory if I ever get close to the summit." I finally got it across that the flag had to be made of silk or a similar material, extremely light and as wind- and weather-resistant as possible.

In a special pocket in my backpack I'm carrying a good deal of logo flags and odd items. All precious cargo. I have deliberately not faced how many flags I'll actually have to carry at high altitude. Fundraising first—then the practical troubles.

O

The champagne is having the desired impact. Slowly I am beginning to relax. At last, at least as long as I'm in the air, no problems can catch up with me. That is, if the plane stays in the air. Ha! That would be a joke! Unwinding a little, I leave the money transfer problems behind— till Kathmandu.

Maybe, just maybe, inner calmness will pervade me before the strain starts anew in Kathmandu. But because of the rush and stress I've lived with—for too long—it's probably going to take an extended period of hibernation before I regain some sense of harmony. Some day—after Everest . . . The influence of the Sherpas will help me get back on track.

Over the chicken and some wine, my seatmate and I timidly start to communicate. It turns out that he normally doesn't travel business class either. We are having a cozy time, exchanging perceptions of our fortune and awkwardness regarding our upgrading. He knows nothing of mountaineering and Everest, but is on his way to Bangkok to offer know-how to a Thai environmental project. We chat about the explosive development in Asia, my work in Greenpeace and how much he is looking forward to his wife and two kids joining him for two weeks' holiday. The manner in which he speaks about his family—his impossible teenage son and lovely daughter—adds fuel to my urge for children.

In his suitcase my seatmate carries a small plastic bag containing Danish snowdrops and anemones—a gift to a dear friend who wants to plant them in his garden, far away from home, in remembrance of his home country. The frail flowers make me wistful. I have been so busy getting to this point that I didn't find time to enjoy the snowdrops pushing their heads through the winter cover. I recall a certain place in my local park where the ground is covered with anemones I will not have the chance to enjoy.

At Bangkok, we part without having exchanged names, I pondering part of my Everest mantra—"and safe return"—so that I will have the chance to enjoy what he has. So that I, in time, can please a faraway friend with snowdrops and anemones rooted in a clod of earth.

At Bangkok's airport I start tensing up again. What will happen when I land in Kathmandu? Has Karen really succeeded in having my name dropped from the climbing permit—and what is Scott's part in this mess?

Thank God I was thinking ahead and got the name of the hotel where our expedition members are supposed to gather during the next three days. If neither Scott nor P.B. picks me up at the airport to help me through the impenetrable Nepalese bureaucracy, at least I know where to head.

The universe of humans often seems menacing, full of conflict stemming from people's own inner dramas, little wars that have nothing to do with me, but which are likely to affect my well-being. That's when I withdraw from the world into the simplicity of the mountains . . . to peace.

Arrival: Kathmandu

No Mountain Madness crew at the airport. Luckily I'm a big girl now and accustomed to taking care of myself. Gather up two bulky 110-liter Lowe expedition duffels (easy to spot with their Netto and *Ekstra Bladet* logos*—yet another way I raised funds), a 70-liter backpack and a 40-liter daypack with all my photo equipment. Tomorrow I'll have to find the cargo storage and waste hours getting my remaining two bags released from customs.

My feet hurt. Among other "infirmities," I suffer from squashed fore-feet, as the specialist so thoughtfully brands what I thought were bunions; stress only makes my collection of disabilities worse.

Wow! It's warm here. Maybe even eighty degrees, but not at all the heat wall you hit stepping out in Bangkok.

I try hard to kick my brain into functioning mode. Do I have to declare the expedition gear? My money belt contains a great deal more than the allowed amount, but following Scott's example—he stuffs enough dollars into his boots and Starbucks Thermos to pay for the whole expedition—I march through innocently: "Nothing to declare." No problem!

Himalaya—why has it taken me so long to come back to you? Here, where I discovered the peace in humans, the peace I was seeking on my travels to foreign parts. Where the land itself radiates peace. Where the highest mountains in the world do something unfathomable to us.

---

*Netto is a major European grocery chain; *Ekstra Bladet* is Denmark's largest daily newspaper in tabloid format.

MARCH 24, 1996

Just arrived at Hotel Manang in the Thamel, Kathmandu's tourist district. The bathroom is quite luxurious by Nepalese standards, but the water from the taps is more turbid than clear. It's a dubious enterprise to clean oneself in Kathmandu water, let alone ingest it. So, from now on, bottled water only for drinking and brushing teeth. Four to eight liters for every twenty-four hours.

Kathmandu seems unchanged—and, yet, a touch of the calm ambiance is lost with the recent wave of Indian immigrants, who seem to be rather insistent salesmen. Worth pondering. What has always captivated me is the sincerity and proud tranquility displayed by the Sherpas. It's better to be a genuine friend than greedy.

Scott's here, showing me the latest news from the Mountain Madness front. Karen has sent him a vehement document in which she asserts that I am a liar and a fraud. I'm glad I had the foresight to bring all the documentation with me to substantiate my claims. Because Scott knows me, he trusts me—or so he says and looks as if he means it. A pretty tense setup, facing Manomi and Jane Bromet, two newcomers to Mountain Madness. They will participate on the trek to Base Camp.

P.B. Thapa calls. We will all meet for dinner tonight, invited by a Swiss lady. Wonder what P.B. thinks. He hasn't seen me since 1991, and now he's bombarded with faxes from Karen, accusations that, mildly speaking, put me in a bad light. At the same time he's the one with the climbing permit in hand. I appreciate my experience, which helps me remain composed, trusting that the mere fact that I am definitively here will cause Karen to work extraordinarily hard to get a handle on the bookkeeping and find my money transfers.

Scott is ill—he's coughing and has a fever. I feared as much after his recent letters. He's pushing himself too hard and doesn't rest thoroughly between his big trips. Hmmm! I guess that leaves me to participate in the "support team"; we'll have to see what results my cocktail of vitamins can have on the effects of high-altitude mountaineering. I only wish my Tai Chi teacher could have worked with Scott more intensely when he was in Copenhagen. Perhaps Scott could have grasped the necessity of relaxing deeply—just now and again.

Scott just spoke to his wife and two kids back in Seattle. "I miss them," he says, but it never makes him stay home for very long, a fact I have touched on in our correspondence. Unfortunately I know what damage an absent father can do to his kids. But, taught by bitter experience, I know it's none of my business. People's private lives are their own domain. Actually, I find it hard to picture Scott being fulfilled if he were not being adventurous. He seems to have too big an appetite for life to live any other way.

O

I am dependent on books, and Kathmandu is a true paradise for bookworms. A good selection at reasonable prices can be found. The subjects of mountaineering and Buddhism, in particular, are richly represented, and I spend hours browsing the tiny shops. Today I find Chris Bonington's book *Quest for Adventure* and *On Top of the World* by Rebecca Stephens, the first British woman to climb Everest by the route we'll be taking.

My focus has changed since I was last here; I've grown over the years and now express different aspects of my personality. Then I was on the verge of a spiritual awakening and was only just beginning to feel attracted to Buddhist literature. But the way of the Sherpas has done something to me. And now—I smilingly state—I am moving from scaling inner heights to ascending outer ones.

I buy several expedition accounts and biographies—to learn from others' experiences and to recognize myself in their quests for adventure. Reading about mountaineering is getting dull because it's becoming obvious how uniformly we think, express ourselves and are driven by recognizable inner forces. In "our universe" we are the norm, and the others are those that do not understand. We don't ask why we do it. Nor do we admire. That's just the way it is.

O

"Lene, this is Anatoli Boukreev, the Russian climber." At our expedition dinner, Jane introduces me to one of the guides.

Ah! *This* is Anatoli. He seems unobtrusive, almost shy or timid. Blond, about five feet ten inches tall. No conspicuous bundle of muscles. Reminds me of the farmer's son from my early youth by the North Sea. He's obviously uneasy about the slightly formal atmosphere— we're all behaving civilly for our Swiss host.

"Anatoli, weren't you on Dhaulagiri spring of '91, making the first ascent on the West Wall?"

"How did you know?"

"I recognize you as one of the Russians who donated your vodka to us, the night we spent in bivvy bags outside your camp. Don't you recall four women climbing up the glacier moraine in early evening? We hiked out from Dhaulagiri Base Camp? I even have some photos of you."

"Hmmm!"

That meeting apparently left no trace in Anatoli's memory.

"Later on we met again when the Danish Dhaulagiri expedition celebrated Jan Mathorne's thirtieth birthday at Rum Doodle. You brought him a bottle of vodka as a present, and I got your address in case I ever had the opportunity to climb Khan Tengri in your home country. And now it turns out that not only do you know Scott, but you're also a good friend of Michael Jørgensen."

"Yes, Michael and I became friends on Everest last year. He is strong. He will climb on Henry Todd's expedition this year, trying to summit without oxygen from the south side this season, and climb Lhotse after.* And you want to be the first Danish woman to summit Everest?"

"Yes, I'm eager to give it a try."

"Why do you want to climb? You are a woman!"

Here I am among the elite of mountaineers—including this thirty-eight-year-old Russian who has summited more mountains than any Danish lowlander could ever dream of—and he asks me why I feel driven to climb that mountain! Another code obviously operates in Anatoli's world, but I'm accustomed to that code and that type of response, and have nearly forgotten my past battles on that account. I need not answer, need not fight to prove anything. All I want is to get to the top of Everest. And talking won't get me there. Only the actual climb will reveal whether I've got it or not. So I keep my mouth shut. I, too, want to find out if I am capable of what, deep inside, I believe I can accomplish. But visions have to be transformed into reality, otherwise they are nothing but illusion. And I hate it when people talk but never do. I have to be careful not to give in to that intoxicating habit myself.

---

*Jørgensen was the first Dane to reach the top of Everest, from Tibet in 1995.

"Now I know who you are," Anatoli says. "I recognize you now—you competed for the world championship in bodybuilding, correct?"

The guy's got a sense of humor! He clearly hasn't got a clue that he's already met me several times, but as a professional he has obviously evaluated my bulk. According to his verdict, all my hard training has paid off. Makes me glad.

I keep in good condition by doing Tai Chi, pushups and situps and by jogging, biking and climbing, and I am usually fanatic about not becoming overweight, so it's been quite a project to improve my survival odds by gaining weight for Everest.

Above 16,400 feet, the human body degenerates steadily, no matter how much one consumes or how much one rests. From 19,700 feet and up, the organism deteriorates at an alarming rate, so the extra weight is just one of the ways I've prepared for the upcoming hardships. As a rule, a human can survive a maximum of five days above 26,000 feet—the so-called death zone. No matter what you do.

But it is wonderful to eat absolutely anything I fancy. "Dessert? Yes, please." And coffee with cake twice a day. Fat alone is not going to do the job, however, so all that increased intake has been transformed into muscle by increased daily workouts.

My weight is now around 155 pounds, but if the Kathmandu "quick-step"—the two-way runs—catches up with me, as it does with almost every traveler in Nepal, I'll be down to 150 before leaving the city.

I've caught myself standing in front of the mirror, disliking those extra pounds, but I comfort myself by thinking that the mirror in two months' time ought to tell a different story—if things turn out! If for no other reason, I will climb that mountain to avoid having to go on a diet on my return. What a horrible thought!

Here, I'm among some of the best mountaineers in the world, and I will be carefully evaluated on my performance. Have I done enough? The competition here is very different from that back home in little Denmark, where it's not hard to rank as a mountaineer. Climbers are not what we breed in our country—one of the flattest in the world—surrounded by water and totally off the map to any climber with the slightest self-respect.

My plan is to climb without supplemental oxygen. Those who have summited Everest without using bottled oxygen have certain physiological advantages that can't be completely predicted by measuring the climbers' physical capacities at sea level. They have an extraordinary ability to perform physically hard work over extended periods of time, an efficient, swift climbing technique that wastes as little energy as possible, a high level of oxygen intake through the lungs and normal or increased breathing response to oxygen deprivation, or hypoxia. Add to that, effective functioning of the muscles during hypoxia and the ability to think constructively despite insufficient oxygen supply to the brain.*

Apart from my desire to summit Everest, I know I am an asset to the well-being of the expedition. Scott invited me to be part of the Mountain Madness team. I don't think he knows what it is that I do that works on trips, but he notices that it makes a difference whether I am there or not. I know I am good at making a group function, partly

---

*The atmospheric pressure on the summit of Everest is one-third of that at sea level. So on the summit of Everest, the oxygen pressure of body tissues is about one-third of the oxygen pressure at sea level—leading to all the physiological changes that follow when the body is starved of oxygen. To a certain extent, the body can gradually adapt to increased altitude and the resulting lower levels of oxygen—a process called acclimatization—but it can take a month or more of gradual ascent.

because of my work as a therapist but mainly because I care about people and it makes me happy if I can contribute to creating a whole that is bigger than the sum of its parts. Now that we have to spend two months of our lives attempting to climb this mountain together, why not try to make the best of it?

That can be quite a project, actually, as many expeditions are not that humane, once you peep behind the "heroic" façade normally presented to the press, among others, a façade that may cover some pretty horrifying facts. In mountaineering, as in life, one should not necessarily trust surface appearances.

All this pondering is interrupted by Anatoli's mumbled good-bye as he vanishes from the party, setting out on his own paths in Kathmandu.

I instinctively like him and must admit that his English has improved considerably since our last encounter, when I judged him "indoctrinated and inarticulate." I enjoy it when life teaches me that I can be very obstinate and critical and haven't got a clue about the truth. Serves me right!

MARCH 25, 1996

The plane from the States is delayed, meaning it will be several days before the remaining members of the expedition arrive. Consequently, we'll be delayed departing Kathmandu. That affects the overall schedule, so P.B. must rebook the helicopter from here to Syangboche. Originally, we were to fly in to Lukla on one of the tiny propeller-driven planes, which is a harsh enough altitude gain. At the last minute, it's been decided that we'll fly by helicopter directly to the airstrip above Namche Bazaar at 11,300 feet (3,450 m)—and that's high! Guaranteed headaches and altitude sickness because of the abrupt ascent. I am not enthusiastic, but it saves two days' yak transport of our expedition gear and, therefore, a neat sum of cash.

My morning was spent picking up the remaining two expedition duf-fels. P.B. was to help me, and after finally finding him, the three-hour-long bureaucratic theater I had so prayed to be spared began: papers to be picked up here, stamped there and copied elsewhere, far away in the outskirts of the city. P.B. has more urgent matters to get under control, so I am turned over to his brother-in-law, who smiles will-ingly, but lacks any understandable English. We take a moped-ricksha to the cargo halls, even though I try to convince the sweating driver, in vain, that there is no way my expedition gear will fit into his tiny car. The driver and the brother-in-law keep smiling, so I leave events to their course.

At the cargo halls, approximately five guys are preoccupied with the necessary paperwork to get my two duffels released. A youthful lad, evidently climbing the bureaucratic ladder, drags me into a shed, where an elderly official stamps every single parchment-like docu-ment. Nobody speaks any English and, embarrassingly, I still haven't learned Nepali. "How much is it?" or the word for popcorn probably won't get me very far here. Now they vanish up some stairway, and somebody mutters "Police."

Giggling overwhelms me as I remember tales of the hassle it takes to get an expedition in and out of Nepal: the rupees needed to help the process run smoothly, and all the neat, accurate paperwork that, after all the bother, faces a good chance of ending up at the bottom of a stairwell serving as a well-deserved feast for the holy cows. A digni-fied manner of filing paperwork!

Another guy signals me to follow him to yet another "official," the boss himself this time, who is in charge of handing out the cargo an-swering the description on the documents. My biggest nightmare is that some of my luggage hasn't made it. Each item was laboriously selected and packed, and is vital for the completion of this climb. Nothing superfluous, nothing dispensable. Well, apart from a pair of bottle-green lace underwear I've brought as a tribute to my womanliness. From my previous trips, I know that an immense urge to wear feminine clothes will engulf me when the hardships are over.

"Passport photos?"

"Yeah." Thank God I brought extra.

We now venture into another hall and into a jumble of people, more people in one space than I am used to. To me the tight gathering seems threatening; the locals, I'm sure, find it comforting. The only other women in the hall are a Japanese mother and daughter. Boxes and wrapped goods are everywhere, piled from floor to ceiling. My courage falters—how on earth will they find my two packs in this mess?

Time passes, and, for something to do, I saunter outside onto the porch. I am greeted by many long stares. I have never felt threatened traveling in Nepal. The Nepalese are very respectful, plus they're so little that a huge Danish machine like myself could probably take on a couple at a time. But that would never be necessary, as the spiritual mixture of Hinduism and Buddhism in Nepal makes it an easy and comfortable country to travel in as a foreign woman. In Islamic Pakistan, on the other hand, I had to be constantly vigilant about my behavior, wear local attire and be escorted by a man at all times in public.

I'm gazing at the Taiwanese expedition's plastic barrels, and at their expedition leader, who's counting and double-checking the barrels. Their expedition's aim is a double climb of Annapurna and Dhaulagiri in western Nepal. I smile, not envious, because I'm off to my own adventure.

Finally my duffels are released. Proud and content, I joyfully unlock them so that the supervisor can check the expedition gear I have listed on the numerous documents against the released cargo.

"Where are you going?"

"To Everest."

"Trekking to Base Camp?"

"No. I am going to the summit."

Do you all hear me? I am actually on my way—to the summit of Mount Everest!

The faithful moped-ricksha driver has been patient to get my business. We fight the 250 pounds of luggage into the tiny cabin, with me on top, and return to Hotel Manang, dropping off the brother-in-law at the airport terminal to inquire about news on the overdue expedition members.

Though the plane delay means a lot of scheduling problems for the expedition, it suits me perfectly, handing me a chance to rest for a couple of days after the hectic sponsor hunt and overwhelming attention from the media. I will be needing all my strength, so I carefully consider where to eat lunch today, to minimize the risk of the ever-lurking Kathmandu quickstep.

Ingrid Hunt, our expedition doctor and a very serious young woman, states: "About the probability of catching the runs while you're in Nepal, I'd say: You either have it, or you'll get it!" Unfortunately, my previous experiences indicate she's right. Moreover, it's been three months since Ingrid worked here for half a year, and she's only recently recovered her full strength.

Ingrid and I are having lunch in one of Kathmandu's green oases, a tropical garden in the midst of noisy, teeming Thamel. Ingrid relates meeting Dr. Igor Gamow, the man who invented the Gamow bag, a cigar-shaped, portable hyperbaric chamber. In a brilliantly simple system, an altitude-stricken victim is placed inside the nylon chamber, and air is pumped in with a foot pump. The combination of increased air pressure and oxygen simulates a lower altitude. Our expedition has a Gamow bag, as does Henry Todd's. The two bags will be shared on Everest by all the teams. One will be at Base Camp; the second at Camp II. These orange bags could be the margin between living and dying.

O

Manomi calls my room, and we meet for tea at the roof terrace. She talks about Karen's attitude toward me—she's decided that it's Karen who's on the wrong track. What a relief. She gives me information on Mountain Madness that will be useful for our eventual long-term cooperation. For some time Scott and I have been working on a business vision: I will summit Mount Everest with no O's as part of Scott's expedition. After that it will be easier for me to work as part of Mountain Madness and for the company to gain access to the European market.

O

I practice Tai Chi while looking out at Kathmandu. Too hazy and polluted to glimpse any mountains.

I am focused. Balanced.

Jane comes to my room, bringing Nike hiking shoes and a T-shirt. I tried in vain to convince Nike in Denmark to sponsor training gear and jogging shoes, but Scott was more successful in the States. Most of the training gear, we agree, will be transferred to our climbing Sherpas—they need it more than we do. Especially Lopsang, who's been promoted to sirdar, in charge of the climbing Sherpas. Lopsang's been infected by Western ideals, so he now looks like a rock star, with his long black ponytail, golden earrings (three—one for every time he has summited Everest) and gorgeous face.

P.B. has invited Scott, Jane, Manomi and myself to a "Good luck, friendship" ceremonial dinner in his home, where we are introduced to his wife and three daughters. Manomi and Jane distribute the presents they have brought from the States, and then the women serve small Nepali delicacies.

P.B. is an outstanding cook and has spent the afternoon preparing a meal in our honor in between phone calls to keep control of every expedition detail. A remarkable, pleasant man. Scott teases him by calling him Buddha, but there's something to it. P. B is eternally smiling, gentle and immensely competent. He can make anything happen when he charges out on his motorbike with his briefcase atop the petrol tank.

Tonight P.B. is telling us about the years he's worked with Mountain Madness. When he reveals his dream of someday having the opportunity to study under a Buddhist lama, I inquire if he is acquainted with the Chinese book of wisdom *I Ching*, the book of changes.

"I keep a copy on my bedside table," he answers.

That initiates an honest talk about spirituality. P.B. is a believer. Jane recounts the inexplicable experiences that took place when her mother died. Manomi is originally from Sri Lanka, so nothing ethereal is peculiar for her. I tell them a little about the experiences and change of life perspective I've had in the past few years. Scott is silent.

Jane, whose primary job is to promote Scott and Mountain Madness—she will be filing daily reports on the expedition for *Outside Online*—discusses promoting me worldwide via the Internet.

I'm thinking: "All I want is the summit—and to do it without oxygen! I want to storm onto the international climbing scene, and I'm gonna do it!" I allow myself to be this megalomaniacal only in my thoughts, though.

P.B. winds up the evening by revealing to me a vision he's had: "You will reach the summit. You are strong." At least his words convince me that I have his confidence, and that is important for our future cooperation.

MARCH 26, 1996

My feet are so ugly, and they torment me! I want beautiful, healthy feet! "Sherpa-feet" tease the Americans. I have tried to convince them that healthy feet are broad.

Ate breakfast with Manomi, Scott, and Henry Todd of Edinburgh, leader of the expedition my fellow Dane, Michael Knakkergaard Jørgensen, will climb with. Henry Todd is the main oxygen supplier for Everest this year—the link between Russian manufacturers of bottled oxygen and our expedition. He is tall, full-bearded and resembles a British author more than a mountaineer. His sophisticated use of language entertains me.

Todd wants to know what drives me. He starts talking about Alison Hargreaves, whom he knew for more than ten years: "It had to happen—her climbing careerism. I couldn't really get in touch with her in the end. Last year on Everest, all she could talk about was equipment and climbing. Whenever I made an effort to talk about other topics, she succeeded in avoiding that and getting back to mountaineering and details on the gear. During the ten years I knew her, I was able to hug her only once. We all knew she was going to die in that race."

Having read Alison's book, *A Hard Day's Summer*, I'm inclined to admit that Todd is right. But I never met her, and her climbing performance was absolutely awe-inspiring.

Henry Todd is an outspoken advocate of supplemental oxygen. "Prepare yourself to climb with oxygen," he persuades. "It'll do the trick when you're lying up there at 8,000 meters and a storm's beating through the South Col. Your legs are in the air to keep the tent poles from collapsing, you're freezing your ass off and are about to give in, but then you grab your oxygen mask, and warmth spreads through your body, the uncontrollable shiver of your carcass subsides and you are in heaven."

I'm not really paying too much attention to Todd. The slightest doubt creeping in might crumble my intention to climb without supplemental oxygen. I'm thinking about Michael Jørgensen and his declared ambition to climb Everest, as well as Lhotse, without oxygen—hard-core to hold on to that if you are climbing with an expedition leader and friend who's an oxygen devotee.

The fact that human beings are capable of surviving and functioning at 18,000 feet and that a few have the physiology to endure 29,028 feet—altitudes at which unacclimatized persons would lose consciousness and die—proves how adaptable the human body is. If you acclimatize properly, the body responds by increasing the respiratory rate, lung artery activity, heartbeat and production of red blood cells and hemoglobin, allowing the blood to carry more oxygen. At the same time, alterations in the body's tissue allow it to function under lower oxygen pressure.

The convictions of one's companions sneak up on you though; through osmosis, they gradually change you. So it's easier to be with Scott because he's basically a no O_2 type, even if the rest of the expedition is planning to climb with oxygen. I'm trying to make him follow their example. He's the expedition leader and ought to be on top of the situation, and he has summited previously without O_2 so his ego knows he can do it. But, this once, it would definitely be better for his brain to be spared.

"I don't know, Lene. It's an ego thing," Scott says, grinning.

Scott and Henry are coordinating the Lhotse permit. It's the absolute last chance to sign up before Henry is off for the ministry. My ego stirs. I'd so like to bag two 8,000-meter peaks this season! I'm so damned ambitious, but, Lene, control that drive and stick to one goal: the highest mountain in the world!

My most important task today is obtaining protective envelopes for sending articles and film to *Ekstra Bladet*—and completing the first article from Kathmandu. *Ekstra Bladet* is one of my sponsors. The deal is, I deliver four articles with my own photos from our Everest expedition, and *Ekstra Bladet* gets exclusive rights to the story on the newspaper's front page. A satisfying sum of money was paid in advance—no problem!

The truth be known, *Ekstra Bladet* was not the paper I had hoped for. I don't read it myself, and I had concerns about how a tabloid would use the story. But when I pitched the exclusive rights to the story of "Lene Gammelgaard, the first Scandinavian woman to attempt to summit Everest" to the newspaper world, the other papers were either uninterested, skeptical, "on holiday" or noncommittal: "Try again in a week's time," or "Our experiences with mountaineers have not been too good, but as you're the first woman to try, send a written application and we might consider it."

Ekstra Bladet, on the other hand, took action. My contact, Rud Kofoed, and I met, I mentioned my price and Rud had a brief look at my scribblings. I was curious whether my writing style would be a good "fit" for *Ekstra Bladet*.

"We'll let you know as soon as possible."

So be it.

Not long after, we had a grand meeting at Queen's Pub—a fruitful meeting that inspired confidence in me that these people could make things happen. When *Ekstra Bladet* says yes, there is no small talk. We came up with *Ekstra Bladet*'s contribution to the summit. It would be a plastic-coated mock front page of the paper announcing my summit success. Three days later, they had produced a mockup with my face plastered all over it. Date: May 8, 1996.

Ekstra Bladet turned out to be a tremendous business partner. And, most important, good people. Not snobbish, made of flesh and blood. I liked visiting the paper. Cozy. Yet another prejudice felled. But isn't that delightful! During my sponsor chase, I came to realize that I go for sponsors I can sympathize with as people, and ones who dare to act—to make things happen.

MARCH 27, 1996

Yes! The remaining members of our expedition finally began arriving yesterday, so we are booked on the helicopter for early morning, March 29. The unified Sagarmatha Environmental Expedition gathered in the lobby this morning. We are a strong team—no doubt about that.

Initially I was introduced to Pete and Klev Schoening. Scott's very proud and happy about their participation. "They are a major contribution to our team, don't you think?"

Having stood at navel's height, gazing up, up, trying to find the end of Klev, and having spoken to both Schoenings, I'm convinced they are. A remarkable pair, these powerful gentlemen. Meeting them reminds me of my "petiteness." These guys are stronger than all the training in the world could ever make me. Mixing with the elite, I feel a touch of insecurity. It's out of the question I can ever carry as much weight, for as far a distance, as they can. Nature sets its limitations. Now I'm looking forward to meeting Charlotte Fox and Sandy Hill Pittman. We might team up, to kind of equalize things.

Charlotte turns out to be slightly taller than I am, and if she's put on weight for Everest, I dare not picture what her normal shape is. Her friend Tim Madsen is a little guy. Charlotte grins as she states, "There's no way I could allow myself to weigh more than my boyfriend." Tim decided to come at the last minute. He has no high-altitude experience, but rumor has it he's an all-around top athlete.

Sandy, I learn, had summited the highest mountain on six of the seven continents. She has spent hours in body-building centers; I recognize the distinct rounded musculature. She's got short dark hair, and her assertive attitude sometimes makes me slip and think to myself "Pit bull" instead of "Pittman."

"If you don't mind, please step outside so I can shoot some photos for my diary on the Internet, and if you could briefly introduce yourself on this tape recorder, I'll have my secretary type it up."

Red light, full stop! "Sandy, the letter you distributed on your media project said we could participate if we wanted to. And I'm not sure I want in."

Will my response trigger a struggle for the upper hand? Guess it's good we're from different countries, for what can a newcomer from Denmark mean to her? But we are here to climb this mountain together, so I find no incentive to cultivate these private feelings.

Martin Adams doesn't attract any attention in the beginning, and it takes a while before I manage to get his and Tim's names right. At first, all I can remember is that the two not-so-big guys are Tim and Martin, but which one is Tim, and which one Martin?

Neal Beidleman is absent. He's the unfortunate one whose duffel disappeared during the plane delay, and, among other important items, his high-altitude down suit is missing. Neal has decided to stay behind in Kathmandu till his gear shows. He's got a cough like Scott's and claims, as Scott does, that it's got nothing to do with the consequences of high-altitude climbing.

Dale Kruse I know from several previous trips—we met up again in Pakistan and not long ago in Ouray, Colorado, where we had a fantastic training week, scaling frozen waterfalls together.

"Hey, man, new glasses. Fancy!"

We'd been teasing him in Colorado. Dale is tall and quite a handsome man, but he stored his looks behind a dull pair of dark glasses. And here he is, displaying smart glasses that truly complement his masculine face. Dale hands me a letter from his wife, Terry, who's become a good friend. We tackled some routes together during the last weekend in Ouray. She is strong and a blessing to be with.

Terry and I first met on a summer hike in Pakistan and quickly found each other's company enjoyable. Several times Dale and Terry have invited me to river raft with them, and one evening, Terry introduced me to a skill crucial for handling the rivers, namely, the art of drinking red beer—consisting of a can of beer mixed with tomato juice. On a long rafting trip, it's impossible to have enough cold beer, but beer blended with tomato juice apparently can be consumed at any time regardless of temperature.

I'm aware of Terry's mixed emotions about Dale's participation in this expedition, but I respect that she has not upset his apple cart. She has abstained from climbing this time: "I've chosen to make my job the priority and think more of the future than I used to," she writes.

Scott arrives with good news: "Karen woke me up at twelve o'clock last night; all checks and transfers have arrived." That's settled, then.

Later I make my ritualistic tour to Pashupati to watch and photograph the Hindu cremations. Manomi decides to accompany me. Getting acquainted with some essential sights of Kathmandu will help her when she returns to the States to sell treks.

Joint dinner at the hotel in one and a half hours. Happy. Happy to be here. Happy to be part of this strong team. Thanks, Scott, for giving me this opportunity!

MARCH 28, 1996
Departing tomorrow morning. I'm excited and must reorganize my gear. Won't need the three bags of high-altitude gear until Base Camp,

so shipped the lot off for yak transportation. That leaves one bag with everything I need for the hike in, plus the backpack with my two cameras, Nikon F90X and Nikon FM2, and an abundance of film. Relatively new for me to be dealing with picture-taking on a more professional level, but have fallen in love with the two cameras and the lenses for every occasion. Getting to know them a bit. I'm pretty well organized actually—planned ahead, so not much to repack. Lopsang gets a fleece jacket, and the Netto T-shirts have already been distributed among the climbing Sherpas. Goggles, intended for Scott, go to Lopsang.

Our team was to have dinner with Sandy Pittman—NBC invited us, but for unknown reasons the plan got quashed. Instead I enjoy an exquisite dinner with Pete and Klev Schoening. A rare privilege sharing their presence. We mention neither mountaineering nor our impending trip to Everest, but talk instead of life, Pete's experiences as a businessman and Klev's solid family network. The two gentlemen insist on taking care of the bill, and I feel very much like a woman.

I know from Scott that Pete, who belongs to a different era of mountaineering, is skeptical about having women on the expedition. During the preparations for this adventure, I was, for a long time, the only woman, but within the last few months, Charlotte and Sandy joined in. In spite of his skepticism, I detect no disapproval from Pete.

P.B. calls. "I cannot find Scott. Departure time has changed—we must be ready to leave the hotel at 5:45." I begin to hunt down the others, leaving messages when people are not available, calling those in the hotel. Neal informs Dale and Ingrid, who've chosen to stay at Hotel Garuda.

Yes! It's happening! I make a vow to myself to enjoy every step of this adventure—to the summit and safe return. Good night!

Namche Bazaar

MARCH 29, 1996

Fifty minutes by helicopter. How easy to fly through the air compared to the hard drudgery of trekking! Perfect—landing in the middle of paradise. Sunny, warm and, so far, no altitude problems. P.B. had just enough time to recount the night's happenings before we departed Kathmandu. He had been informed that our helicopter pickup was two hours earlier and had raced around all night to ferret out the nine climbing Sherpas. Few have telephones, so he had to drive to the different homes, families and girlfriends, till he found Lopsang and could assign him to the project. P.B.'s efforts prove fruitful, because everyone shows, and on some chests I catch a glimpse of black letters spelling out Netto on a yellow background—the Sherpas' T-shirts!

Charlotte, Sandy and I gather, tittering, discussing our "increased body mass." Typical women! Sandy had her secretary buy the most outrageous bikinis for the team ladies. Intended for "before" and "after" pictures at Base Camp. Why not? Jokes are well suited to the lunacy we're headed for. Feels great to have a thorough laugh, to get rid of all the accumulated tension.

We eat lunch at P.B.'s. Doctor Ingrid advises us against eating meat, but I *must* order mixed momos, Nepali-style spring rolls which contain yak meat and local vegetables. Charlotte orders a club sandwich; she's courageous to challenge anything that exotic. She goes down big time soon after. Tim describes her condition when we empathetically inquire how his love is doing: "It comes out both ends, and fast!" What an accurate description . . .

At P.B's I discover an expedition postcard: Henrik Jessen Hansen, Bo Belvedere, Jan Mathorne and Kim Sejberg. So the four Danish guys have been through here recently. Actually pretty impressive gathering from Denmark this season. Four guys on one team, Michael Knakkergaard Jørgensen on Henry's team and Lene Gammelgaard on Scott's Sagarmatha Environmental Expedition. As far as I know, no Dane has challenged Everest from the Nepal side since Claus Becker Larsen's adventurous but illegal attempt—entering the area without a permit—in 1951. And now six Danes are going for the summit. Not bad!

I've been sitting for hours on a flat sunny stone next to the Tengboche trail. My respiratory rate increased after arriving at this altitude (Namche is 11,300 feet above sea level); after several days here, it will stabilize at a more harmonious level. I became fatigued and out of breath as I slowly, slowly climbed the steep path to where I rest now. I trust, though, that those problems will improve as my body acclimatizes. I also realize that for the next months at high altitude, I will be exposing my system to extreme stress and pressing myself to the absolute edge, and that I'll pay with long-lasting fatigue and reduced strength when I return home.

I seek solitude, to connect with inner peace. Tai Chi among the giants of the universe. Belonging. Absolute serenity.

It's worth everything, being here again!

MARCH 30, 1996
Taking it easy, as the direct jump to 11,300 feet requires three to four days of rest, with minimal activity, before you can start working hard. The risk of altitude sickness is huge, and flying in like we did is pressing our luck.

Reports from up-trail of unusual snowfall for the season. Yaks can't get through to Base Camp, and all expeditions seem to be stuck in a traffic jam at Lobuche. The porters want double payment to force their way through the snow masses. Wonder where Anatoli is. He left a couple of days before us, to supervise setting up Base Camp and to prepare for establishing the higher camps. Well, it'll be days until we get that far, and here there's no more snow than usual, though Kathmandu reports knee-deep snow on the landing field.

Jane asks me what my plans are after finishing this expedition. Christ, first I have to survive this climb; then time will tell.

The lodge we're staying at is owned by our Sherpa leader's family. They have given us two of their own rooms as dining space. Houses in Namche are typically two-story buildings, rather spacious, with windows on three walls. On the fourth wall is the home altar. The lower half houses the family collection of fine china; the upper contains brick-size objects wrapped in orange cloth with Buddhist script. I'm guessing they're copies of Buddhist scriptures; first time I've come across a collection in a private home. My guess turns out to be correct: the master of the household comments that these days the ancient language of the scriptures can be deciphered only by learned monks. When an important life event happens, monks gather for week-long ceremonial rituals, reciting the ancient scripts to sanction harvest, birth, weddings . . . How I want to experience this . . .

MARCH 31, 1996

Doctor Ingrid's prophecy caught up with me *and* Doctor Ingrid, with whom I'm sharing a room. Therefore I'm ascending at a snail's pace, more slowly than Dale, Jane and Scott, on today's mission: scaling a close-by ridge. Our goal is to shoot pictures of Ama Dablam and Everest; the advice to "climb high, sleep low" will help our carcasses acclimatize. I struggle up the abrupt track leading from Namche across

Syangboche air strip up toward the ridge.

The others' behavior gets on my nerves, and I take off on my own. The effect of this height is an overall weakening of my capabilities, but in spite of my previous offerings to mountains of stomach content, I can still detect some of my strength. Upwards I crawl over mossy, rocky ground and slippery grass. As a bearing, I'm steering toward a stone shrine, a Buddhist chorten, flying prayer flags on the summit ridge. When I stop to catch my breath, I correct my course accordingly. It's far above me, but Dale managed to get up there yesterday, and his story about the spectacular view fuels my progress, though the going is hard. And if this appetizer seems too much, then what about what lies ahead? Struggling, while simultaneously economizing strength. It's a knife-edge balancing act, building up your physical condition yet not taxing the resources that must be available when it truly counts.

Arriving at the chorten, I realize I've overtaken Jane and Scott. Dale is nowhere in sight. The chorten turns out to be a memorial to Tenzing Norgay, the Sherpa who accompanied Edmund Hillary to the summit of Everest in 1953. "Tenzing, Hillary's friend" is the inscription on the memorial plate.* I shoot a roll of film of the monument—with Everest as the background. Must be a favorable sign that I unknowingly aimed toward this spot. Celebrating the event and myself, I unroll my bivvy bag and snuggle up inside for shelter from the never-ceasing winds. Time for a little snooze above Namche with Everest before me, the comforting chorten next to me and ravens, black flyers of the mountains, above.

At 4:00 P.M., it's high time to head down. Merrily I jump along the ridge, passing row upon row of prayer flags. I am thoroughly happy

---

*Tenzing Norgay's actual place of burial is in Darjeeling.

by the time I join Scott and Jane.

"We spent the afternoon shooting pictures for Nike."

"I have to hurry down," Scott adds, annoyed. "I promised to phone P.B. in Kathmandu at five o'clock." And off he goes at full speed.

Apparently I've recovered from the two-way-runs because I think, *I'll show you*. Rarely do I give in to my innate childishness and competitive inclinations; perhaps today I'm in an especially wicked mood. But I know I'm just as fast as Scott and a better navigator. If he's forgotten since Pakistan, it's time to remind him. In all discretion, of course.

So away I go, descending the precipitous wall, balancing on narrow ledges, admiring the imprints of yak hooves. There's an abundance of pheasant-like birds and one unbelievable blue one, which turns out to be Nepal's national bird, better known as the nine-colored bird. "It means good fortune, that you see it," Lopsang says, when I later ask him what species it was.

Climbing up, jumping down, over and over again, till finally I stand on the verge of the natural amphitheater that holds the Sherpa capital, Namche Bazaar. And then—like the Sherpas—I run with soft, half-bent knees down to the city. In the center of town, I encounter Lopsang.

"Where is Scott?" he asks.

Then I am down ahead of him! Ha ha! Effective exercise.

"Scott's on his way down with Jane. I believe they might have lost their way," I say innocently. "But he told me he had to be down by five to call P.B."

Lopsang, I know, shares my joy in strength. Sherpas admire, respect true strength; it's probably deeply rooted in them—common sense under their life conditions. If a baby doesn't have sufficient strength, it dies young. To survive and live in this harsh environment demands stamina, and no one attempts to breast-feed and keep a child alive if it shows signs of weakness. Resources are scarce and must be invested carefully.

The lodge is overflowing with a South African expedition beset by internal rifts. Even before leaving Namche, some of the members ran afoul of their leader, so they quit and are returning to Kathmandu, where they'll attempt to get the climbing permit altered to their names. One of them is severely sick from the high altitude and is now being transported back to Kathmandu.

So far we have been a magnificent expedition, made up of independent, experienced individuals tried by life events and not easily shattered. A true privilege in comparison with the South African mess and previous climbing experiences I've had.

Dingboche

APRIL 2, 1996

Sonam Friendship Lodge. Hardly trusting I've returned, I barely recognize the lodge. It has been budding in the past five years and has suffered from growing pains. We camp on the field nearby, and it's certainly a relief to finally sleep outside. Because of the snow condition reports from the Khumbu Glacier, we've decided to hike here, to Dingboche, instead of Pheriche as originally planned. Here there's more protection from the freezing winds and fewer expeditions. We need to spend some days at this altitude to acclimate, so the obvious choice was the more pleasant spot, where we'll enjoy the last scraps of vegetation. From here upwards, nothing—no green growth for one and a half months. I am in top form, happy to be here. Tai Chi in the moonlight, honorable people in Pete and Klev.

It's happening again! When I work myself hard, my brain activity is reduced to a minimum. Everything becomes straightforward and simplified. It is no longer possible for me to construct profound, bombastic, philosophical thought patterns or to complicate my life with complex psychological analyses.

Simplicity—it satisfies me. As long as it is not synonymous with being reduced to a state of stupidity. I possess a magnificent book in my home library, *Earthly Happiness* by the Chinese author Lin Yutang. He writes on the pleasures of life:

> *It seems to be destined by fate that I have developed into a sort of market philosopher, nothing to do about that though. Commonly philosophy seems to be this special science that makes plain and uncomplicated matters difficult to comprehend, whereas I readily think of a philosophy that, on the contrary, makes complex matters simple and easily grasped. In spite of such appellations as materialism, humanism, transcendentalism, pluralism and all the remaining lengthy words ending with "ism," I will profoundly insist that these systems are not more firmly rooted than my own private philosophy. When all is said and done, life consists of eating, sleeping, meeting your friends, saying hello to them at social gatherings, farewell parties, in laughter and lament, having a haircut, watering one's plants and witnessing one's neighbor tumble from the roof. Philosophy has, therefore, become a science, by which we increasingly understand less and less of everything that concerns ourselves. On one particular point the philosophers have come far: The more they talk about the problems of existence, the more confused we become.*

Good night and sweet dreams!

APRIL 4, 1996

Another rest day in Dingboche. Mild symptoms of altitude sickness: slight headache, lethargy, somewhat apathetic, no appetite for anything but ramen noodle soup. Strange, I always get a craving for this instant brew when I climb high. Seeking peace, I consider a river bath, but ice covers the stagnant puddles. Believe the cold would be overwhelming for me just now. I have no desire to be with the team. Vegetating and saving energy for Everest. No one expects close contact. We are all in the same boat.

Notes:

Idea for future book project: duality of good and evil. The one who chooses to live a socially correct but superficial life, ending up a shadow of himself; versus the outsider who sinks deeply, explores all levels of life, but reaches the genuine goal in the end . . . Explore how contradictory judgments can be passed on them.

Are certain individuals predisposed to ascribing spiritual values to life's occurrences?

What can you make of "living in the present"? How does it affect people?

O

I am by the river, bathing in stages. The water is cold, but I've given in to my passion for glacier bathing. I simply can't resist close encounters with clear streams of icy, pure water, a phenomenon that has stayed with me since childhood.

When I was in Pakistan, one of my favorite occupations in the afternoon, when the sun had defrosted the glacier rivers, was to pick up my photo equipment and notebook and venture out onto the glacier. Away from any human presence. Finding my way among ice pinnacles and nature's amazing sculptures and attempting to catch these creations with the camera.

Then I'd select the most exquisite point on the ice bank by a stream of meltwater. Typically the water was a foot and a half deep and racing past. What a delight to strip off my clothes and bathe in this Eden of ice and meltwater. Had to watch myself not to let go, and give in to the desire just to flow downriver through this ever-changing universe.

When Scott and I were coming down from Broad Peak Base Camp in 1995, we went astray in a gorgeous desert of crevasses and moraine streams and jumped one crevasse after another and leaped across several glacier streams. One of the streams turned out to be too wide for my jumping technique, and I landed on my ass in the chill water, grinning from ear to ear. That's where I invented a way to fulfill my dream of body rafting down a glacier stream. As it often goes with brilliant ideas, someone had come up with it before me—hydro speed is already popular. Been too hung up to try it—yet!

Today a more normal river grants me serenity. Time heals all wounds, and I have forgotten who I was back then, recalling only enough to appreciate that the mere pain of living is considerably less now. I have learned to be more content. I am where I belong—and I don't necessarily mean here on my way to Everest—but right now I am where I'm supposed to be. My life has a tendency to be extremely inconstant, but I guess I have come to terms with and accepted that my inconstancy derives from a complex personality with innumerable nuances, all of which crave their right to live at some point. As long as

I don't block this inner flow, I'm in harmony.

This sensation of being truly alive, conforming with one's inner flow, is the highest achievement, they say, and metaphor is used again and again to illuminate that experience. The mystics of the Middle Ages said that "the inner God experience was the spring of life," and Zen Buddhists liken the experience of enlightenment to having a drink of water after having been parched by the desert. In every culture, this feeling stands for complete fulfillment, an abundance of life learnings. A core value that crosses religious boundaries.

The rays from the sun warm me up, so I start washing my hair. Winds blow colder now, making me long for the ice landscapes of the Khumbu Glacier.

O

I am happy. We pass the afternoon practicing using the Gamow bag. Jim Litch, a doctor from the high-altitude clinic in Pheriche, participates and shares his experiences with altitude sickness: "High altitude can be deadly. Just take it easy—slowly, slowly—and you'll be okay." The facts boil down to these:

HAPE: High-altitude pulmonary edema. The air sacs of the lungs fill with fluid—literally drowning you in your own body fluids.
Cause: Probably oxygen deprivation and increased pressure in the pulmonary arteries.
Prevention: Gradual ascent.
Treatment: Rapid descent—Go down! Or raise the atmospheric pressure around the victim by using the Gamow bag. More oxygen is the key. The steroid dexamethasone may stop the fluid leakage.

HACE: High-altitude cerebral edema. Fluid leaks from cerebral blood vessels and accumulates inside the skull, causing mental and motor skills to deteriorate. Coma, then death, can occur if the person doesn't descend immediately.

Cause: Oxygen deprivation.

Prevention: Gradual ascent.

Treatment: Same as for HAPE.

My homework becomes real to a different extent out here. I have tremendous respect for the havoc high-altitude oxygen deprivation can wreak on the body. Lots of things you can train for, prepare yourself for, but you cannot control how your body is going to react when its oxygen intake is reduced. All you can do is know the symptoms and react with common sense. That's if you are lucky enough to realize what is happening, because cerebral edema can affect your ability to think and react intelligently and rationally.

Scary stuff!

Some of us will be affected. That's just the way it is, even if at this point we don't know who it will be. Dale has never performed well at altitude and has suffered severe symptoms the past few days. Altitude sickness has forced him to abandon several previous expeditions. I don't get why he spends his energy trying again. We touched on the subject in Colorado, and I inquired, "Why don't you focus on rock climbing instead—or ice climbing?" Dale is as strong as an ox and could literally live out on rock faces. Instead, he suffers defeat again and again because of altitude. If you have suffered from HAPE or HACE on previous trips, you will probably suffer again; on the other hand, never having any appreciable problems is no guarantee you'll go free on your next trip.

Because Dale is tall, we pick him to play "victim" as we practice using the Gamow bag. It's quite a hassle, stuffing a "semiconscious" guy into the cigar-shaped bag, but finally a smiling Dale peeps up through the little plastic window. The oxygen saturation in Dale's blood increases from 75 percent to 98 percent within very few pumps; simultaneously, his pulse decreases. Martin, the appointed pump-man, might soon need an oxygen refill himself after his contribution—it's hard work maintaining a constant, sufficient pressure inside the bag at this altitude, and this leads to more true tales from Jim about transporting altitude-sick victims in the Gamow bag through the Khumbu Icefall.

Scott shares the sweetest story of an earlier test with the Sherpas: "All this shit about atmospheric pressure gets pretty complicated, especially up here, where your brain doesn't get enough O_2. I'm no damn good at explaining the technical details anyway. So I just use my well-developed pedagogical skills to tell the Sherpas what it is that Gamow bags do. I say that if one of them gets sick up at Camp II at 6,500 meters, we can stuff him in the Gamow bag and the effect will be as if he were in Lhasa. A forest of fingers goes up when I ask for a volunteer—they *all* want to go to Lhasa!"

Dale's making himself cozy in his pressure chamber, grinning, displaying the pulse oximeter again and again. This may help him recover a bit from his altitude trouble. Great to establish that our bag functions and, even better, ascertain that our teamwork is excellent. Minor flaws here and there, consequences of the devastating runs, nausea and altitude, but otherwise we're a good team. Strong. Well balanced. And cooperative, as demonstrated by this training session. We're all rather strong personalities and know our own worth, so no one has the opportunity to dominate. We are grownups, bearing the signs of our life experiences, and we're good, inspiring company—each in his or her own way. How privileged to be allowed to be ourselves!

Neal, though, seems a bit out of sync with me. As I see it, he's so wrapped up in his assignment as assistant guide that he occasionally loses touch with the ground. He's commenting on and explaining stuff to me that I learned long ago. It feels patronizing. Scott shakes his head. "Neal, she knows!" I smile, but keep Neal at a distance. I'm not going to Everest to pamper anybody's ego. Apart from my own! If he just steers clear, that's fine with me.

O

In mythology, heroes are characterized by a calling that they embrace without doubt. An adventure hero never considers turning back. There's no discussion: The mission must be completed. As a rule, we humans are beset by competing anxieties—"Should I?" or "Shouldn't I?" "Why?" "Why not?"—and confusion and insecurity lead to inaction. The hero, however, must lead on to the end, even if it includes the risk of death. With that calling, that obedience to an inner authority, the hero symbolizes the human personality with its powers in focus. But people seldom are that focused.

The problem of determining what we are responsible for and where that responsibility stops is one of the dilemmas of existence. Throughout our lives, we are forced to evaluate, and reevaluate, where our responsibilities lie in the constantly changing flow.

Truth is shunned when it is painful or calls for choices we don't want to face. But we must dare to be totally committed to truth. Mental soundness is the continuous process of facing reality as it is, rather than how we wish it to be. To have the courage to live life on life's terms, illusions must be given up. And who does that without a fight?

I'm struggling with my wish to hang on to an idealized vision of Scott, yet I'm confronted with mounting evidence that I can't. I realize that I do not have faith in Scott's capabilities to develop the true professional's breadth of knowledge. I'm glad that I have learned, after many years, to accept the philosophy *trust nobody but yourself* in the extremes of life. But I also realize that Scott has matured since we met in 1991, as I have.

Scott and I are like wild kids—capable of behaving properly, but completely incapable of being controlled by anybody. Inner self-discipline is not what you are best at, Scott Fischer; in that, you're still a youngster.

I'm reading *On Top of the World* about the first British woman who climbed Everest and note the following sentence: "Thanks for being a pathological optimist and for having this diabolic idea in the first place!" Thank God I don't have to convince myself of the saneness of this—because it's not sane!

I am curious how Klev justifies this climb. He seems a very serious man, without a doubt a good family man with sincere respect and genuine love towards his wife and a commitment to his children and business. I'll have to ask him later.

Being a woman and, I hope, a mother someday, I cannot respect men who have kids and simultaneously participate in this deadly game. Maybe the fathers on this team can change my mind. I imagine that when I choose to have children, I will give up my participation in the race to summit the fourteen 8,000-meter peaks. The way I see it now, it's an either/or situation because the risk of dying while climbing is so huge. Just study a few expedition accounts to calculate the odds—they are bad!

Gorak Shep

APRIL 7, 1996

Now we are really getting close to Base Camp. Some snow en route from Lobuche (what a mud hole it's become!), and in spite of the number of yaks that have already passed this way with expedition gear, it continues to be troublesome for them to make any headway. They simply break through the snow crust, sink and are stuck.

The yak herders are often young kids with no other footwear than plastic flip-flops, so it's understandable that they demand extra payment. We crazy foreigners are dependent on a tight schedule to catch the "weather window": a break in the furious storms high on the mountain, mid-May, before the monsoon sets in at the beginning of June. We must get in there to have a chance at the mountain, and we are already running late according to the original schedule, which had us arriving at Base Camp on April 6. But the other expeditions are suffering the same conditions. Wonder where my fellow Danes are? Thought I recognized their yellow fleece long johns this morning outside Lobuche.

O

"Hey, Anatoli! How good to see you again. What does it look like up there? Did our gear arrive? How are the conditions in the Icefall? How many expeditions are there this year?" Questions rain down on the poor Russian, who apparently had had enough of waiting at Base Camp, so away in his sneakers and ski poles he flew, nipping down to Gorak Shep to pay us a visit.

He is remarkable, this man from Kazakhstan. Something about his manner awakens my trust. Not that he tries to be noticed. Anything but! We are gathered outside our tent camp, nice and cozy, listening to Anatoli's answers. I snap photo after photo of his face.

"I don't want my picture taken. No more." Anatoli's dismissal seems fierce.

Yet I carry on. "I'll make you famous in Denmark." Whatever contribution that might be to making life easier for this grand climber.

"Why?"

I honestly don't know. "Maybe you deserve it. How many rolls of film do you have for your camera, Anatoli?"

"Enough."

"How many is that?" I'm forcing myself on him. Why?

"Seven or eight."

"One of my sponsors gave me loads of film; I'll give you some at Base Camp."

"Why?"

Because I have so many, and you so few. That's why. My motherly heart reacts to this man. Nobody knows how intuition operates; sometimes I spontaneously react without knowing if what I'm doing will turn out right or wrong. Towards Anatoli I instinctively react with profound respect and a sort of caring that actually encroaches on the boundaries he has set up. I take more liberties with him than our brief encounter can logically explain. The closer I pay attention to his responses to people's questions, the more my respect grows.

Anatoli gives me a touch of insight into the land he's from. His love for it is infectious. What do I actually know about living in the former Soviet Union? I've spent so much time on Project Everest that I've neglected to cultivate knowledge in other areas.

Jane and Sandy are discussing how to get Anatoli a green card in the States.

"Why? I'm a Russian man."

He's right. Why do we automatically take for granted that Russia is something bad, and that all Russians want to come to the States? Hmmm! Food for thought, though Anatoli is shrewd enough to know what's the best for his future. But he's proud of being Russian.

Wrong, not Russian.

"I am from Kazakhstan. I am a Kazakh man," Anatoli replies shortly and concisely to people's inquiries. He does not speak on his own initiative.

I admire his distinctive hat. A peaked, brightly colored woolen hat with red embroidery.

"It's from my home area. If you ever come there, you can have one."

Anatoli draws back from any further questions about the future with: "First I have to survive this expedition."

Part III

On the Mountain

Everest Base Camp

APRIL 8, 1996

First day in Everest Base Camp and I'm happy about my new home
of ice and snow. Right now it feels as if I'll never get tired of being
here. Can't fathom leaving this place in barely two months. Being here
is the fulfillment of my dreams, and an interruption in life's occa-
sional monotony.

I believe my ability to "conquer" Mount Everest depends on my mental
state. Therefore I must make sure not to have any "bad days." There's
no room for energy-draining conflicts, inner or outer, and bad moods
are something I simply can't afford to waste energy on.

Luckily, I have my secret weapons to bring me into the proper psychological state, that is, when I have the self-discipline to use them.
Tai Chi and contemplation of the *I Ching*, the Chinese book of changes,
calm my spirit whenever the outer world seems too impenetrable or
does not want to behave as I wish. Using these methods I am able to
re-focus and re-establish a peaceful state of mind.

I know that the degree of "success" I attain depends on my inner equi-
librium, and I have learned that my serenity is *my* responsibility. I
decide—to some extent—how my mind reacts to outside events; and
internal mood swings I can control using self-discipline. My honored Tai Chi teacher, Åge, is an annoyingly good teacher. If I showed
up at a training session raw from my job at the drug treatment center, his instructions would be to "concentrate on the training, focus
your energies and remove yourself from whatever is draining your
resources."

His method was highly successful. So, unfortunately, handling my
moods depends on the degree of effort *I* make—to keep my balance,

to not lose my footing, no matter who I am with or where I am.

Scott appears slightly more relaxed now that we have arrived at Base Camp. He seems to have the situation reasonably under control. Our kitchen staff constructed a stone house roofed with bright blue tarpaulin, and it has become the center for Sherpa social life in camp. Ngima, our Base Camp sirdar, is a clever, competent leader. I haven't quite gotten down the names of the individual kitchen Sherpas, but their grinning faces confirm my past yearning to return to Nepal—it wasn't just something I've imagined all these years—the Sherpa people have something. . . .

Our mess tent is assembled—a Russian tunnel tent in three shades of mauve, a good place to return home to, coming down the mountain. Trying to picture how it will look from up on the Icefall, but why don't I simply wait and see.

Behind the mess tent is the communications center—a whole tent of equipment NBC provided to Sandy so that she can make daily reports and be interviewed at the nbc.com website. Wonder how many extra porters she's paid to carry that stuff? Ingrid's clinic takes up one-fifth of the space allocated for the technology. I have mixed emotions about this media circus Sandy seems engulfed by, but as the saying goes, "People in glass houses shouldn't throw stones." Without the power of the Danish press, *I* wouldn't be here. The world is what the world is, and, to an alarming extent, it's controlled by the media. So I either adapt—or . . .

I'm content with the way *Ekstra Bladet* and I agreed to communicate. Our motto: Keep it simple! So technology was overruled; it has a tendency not to function according to plan anyway, complicating matters when you are far from civilization. Instead, I invested in three notepads and plenty of ballpoint pens. Rud will have the delightful task of deciphering my handwriting as the expedition progresses. Our mail runner will take accounts from the ascent down to Namche, where they will go by helicopter freight to Kathmandu, and then, by P.B.'s motorbike, out to our man in the Nepalese department of Wilson Freight; there, modern technology takes over: express delivery to Rud Kofoed and Jan Unger at *Ekstra Bladet*. Possibly within four days!

As for myself, I have arranged it so that no one can contact me except by mail, and that takes at least three weeks. I came here seeking peace and detachment from everything that moves too fast in the modern world.

Next to the kitchen is the storage tent, containing all the expedition gear and food: Italian delicatessen sausages, crackers, rice, pasta, smoked cheese, muesli, beef jerky, turkey jerky, deer jerky, hot chili jerky, smoked jerky, an orgy of sliced dried meats. Those make up the main bulk of our calorie intake here at Base Camp and perhaps at Camp II, but above that we'll live on liquid nourishment—Gatorade, Reeload (argh!) and PowerBars. Also in this tent: climbing rope, snow stakes, oxygen containers, sleeping bags for high camps, the Gamow bag and Jane, who's ferreted out a cozy, warm hollow among the duffels for an afternoon snooze.

O

"Hey, Ngima, do you have an idea when the remaining duffels are meant to arrive? I'm still missing one of my tents and will have a hard time getting settled until I can pitch my mobile home."

"Maybe late today. But we have one runaway yak. Pemba is searching for it."

No problem. I'll just continue clearing away rock and chopping ice at the platform I've chosen for my home base. The various teams' tents are scattered over the glacier, forming a cute village where we're all within seeing and hearing range. I selected a glacier hillock, slightly removed from the main camp, because of its view of the Khumbu Icefall and because I didn't want to be disturbed by noise from other people. It's hard work to shape a platform of ice the size of my tent's ground sheet. Doing my best to stay clear of big rock pieces. The glacier flows constantly and melts during the heat of the day, so sooner or later the rocks may tumble over—preferably not on top of me. Good workout to stagger about with these rocks.

"Strong Danish woman," Anatoli comments from his sunbathing rock. His blue cotton tent, sprinkled with white daffodils, truly brightens this place, like a bouquet of flowers in a bare room, and underscores the difference in the countries we come from. The rest of the expedition's tents are the absolute latest in high-tech expedition gear.

Can't figure out whether Anatoli is being sarcastic or actually means what he says. Can't really be bothered. Time will tell if I'm strong enough to do what I have in mind: To the summit and safe return. No O's!

After all, his evaluation is his. Just because it comes from his mouth doesn't necessarily make it the truth. But support or neutrality are, after all, less energy-demanding than negativity.

The crowning achievement of our camp is a stunning loo, beautifully executed in stone, with high walls on the three sides where "tourists" might pass by. The fourth half-wall faces Pumori, so you can enjoy a view of that peak and the nearby glacier lakes. The sky serves as roof, and the tarpaulin door is fixed to an odd arrangement of strings, so that your dignity is safe even in a stiff gale. The floor is laid with big, flat tiles of rock leaving an opening over a deep, deep hole like an old-fashioned privy. All your business must be done while standing, though.

At first, the hole was too wide—one misstep and you'd vanish down the hole into the growing pile of shit. The construction was improved with splendid results, but they had to raise the floor, so now the upper part of your body sticks up in the open. Rather nice, as you can see if the loo is engaged and by whom.

Toilet paper is available in the mess tent. Valuable sort of paper, any way you look at it. Having an abundance of toilet paper means good trades with less-prepared expeditions later in the season!

My tent arrives, and Krishna smilingly insists on pitching the biggest one—a red Wild Country Couple tent with all the frills, including an indoor drying-net to pitch under the ceiling and extra poles in case of storm damage. Flemming from Ski & Tøj, one of my sponsors, was invaluable in procuring the best possible equipment for me as well as helping me put on weight. He's an excellent chef, the perfect host and a fun traveling companion on the winter training tours to Chamonix. And he's a man of details, so I learned a lot about the latest in mountaineering equipment.

Krishna, a distinctive-looking Sherpa, speaks a bit of English and will remain at Base Camp during the entire expedition. His responsibility—from before dawn till late at night—is providing everything we need as far as food and drink go. He and two other Sherpas rise early, collect water in the nearest glacier pond, heat it and make the morning wake-up rounds to all the tents.

"Good morning. Tea ready." Being woken every morning by a benevolent, smiling boy handing you a mug of steaming hot tea through an ice-covered opening while you are still warm and drowsy in your sleeping bag can easily become an addiction. Must be a holdover from the British era. Coffee is also available. Scott long ago taught our team how to brew strong Starbucks coffee—Seattle-style.

We're all—clients, guides and Sherpas—members of Scott's extended family in the Khumbu region and are treated accordingly. Everybody knows everyone and is in some way or another related. On this trip we have the honor of having Lopsang's father, Ngawang Sya Kya, as one of the high-altitude climbers. Lopsang's father has worked on several Everest expeditions but has never been to the summit, so Scott, being big-hearted, wants to give him the opportunity now.

My own status report on the Sagarmatha Environmental Expedition:

>>Scott's in excellent form, actually better than I've ever seen him, and he's recovered from his cough. No stomach or altitude problems.
>>Anatoli is in super condition. Got here a week before we arrived and is well acclimatized. Good at relaxing when that's what counts.
>>Sandy is in great shape and high spirits, but coughs like a mad-woman. Takes some pretty strong medicine for it and says she feels strong as an ox after she's consumed it. Uses an asthma inhaler at high altitude.
>>Charlotte is in top form. Iron woman. Coughs and has minor troubles with asthma—activity-provoked? Uses an inhaler at high altitude and plans to start taking the same medicine Sandy's taking.
>>Martin is super, but coughs his lungs out during the night.
>>Neal's in great shape. Very fast. Coughs up green slime. Typical for him at high altitude.
>>Tim is in good physical condition. Sleeps. Headache. Some altitude sickness.
>>Dale is in good form. No coughing. No appetite. Headache. Some altitude sickness.
>>Pete is in good shape. Tough guy! His only problem seems to be

insomnia. He can't sleep because of breathing problems. Typical up here: breathing almost ceases at regular intervals. You wake up with a start, breathe deeply and go back to sleep until the next pause. At sea level, oxygen saturation in the red blood cells drops during sleep because of a slight reduction in breathing rate and depth, but the drop is not significant. At high altitudes, the reduction in rate and depth is significant, and inconsistent respiration becomes far more frequent. The deficiency in oxygen this causes is known as sleep hypoxia.* Pete's never suffered from this previously, so a cardiologist—a client on Rob Hall's expedition—offers to carry out some experiments. Pete now uses oxygen to sleep at night, which means he won't have a chance to make a go for the summit.

>>Klev's in super condition. Tough. Calm. But at times he has no appetite; the runs are causing him trouble. He reveals nothing. Klev and Pete are diligent, taking an extra walk each day to train and improve their acclimatization.

>>Myself, I am in great form. High altitude treats me well. After a rather slow start, I'm on an upward curve, under the observant eye of Doctor Ingrid, who keeps a sharp watch for any signs of more serious complications. Have gotten the runs under control, thanks to her, too. I normally leave healing to nature's own pace and course. But Everest is not exactly the body's natural environment, so after a few days "on the run," I opt for the pills so as not to be weakened further.

>>Ingrid makes a strong impression: She's goal-oriented and performs her role as Base Camp manager as well as expedition doctor at full steam. She's also good at braiding my hair into a Heidi "do," a crucial contribution to the successful carrying out of this enterprise.

---

*Sleep hypoxia may also explain why headaches and other symptoms of acute mountain sickness (AMS) are more severe in the morning, and why high-altitude pulmonary edema usually becomes more acute during the night. At sea level, oxygen saturation in the blood cells is 94–96 percent, and oxygen content drops very little during sleep. At 14,000 feet (4,300 m), oxygen content is about 86 percent but can fall to 75 percent with periodic drops to 60 percent.

The dinner gong sounds. The peals from the hanging empty oxygen cylinder mean it's time to haul myself out of the sleeping bag and unplug the Walkman from my ears. Sun's down and it's rapidly getting *cold*. Off with shorts, T-shirt and glacier goggles. On with Helly-Hansen underwear, Feathered Friends long johns—a present from Scott—Lowe Alpine fleece, Gore-Tex shell and a pair of fleece gloves. And to complete the nightly outfit: my "Tibetan wedding hat," a fur-lined, gold-embroidered Tibetan felt hat with long earflaps—truly a gift for keeping the head warm and a genuine means of establishing local rapport—bought in Namche Bazaar in 1991 while trekking in to Island Peak. After stuffing a headlamp and toilet paper in my pockets and throwing a Thermos and a liter plastic flask out of the tent doorway, I start to worm my way over the three duffels blocking my way.

After every meal, the Sherpas fill our containers with boiled water. The Thermos keeps my drinking water from freezing during the night, and I use the boiled water in the plastic flask to warm my feet at the beginning of the night. I'm meticulous about gulping down sufficient fluids—water, tea, juice and water, juice and more water—so I'm always waking up at night to drink and pee. Downing enough fluids helps you acclimatize and is the best preventive measure you can take for altitude sickness.

Everybody knows that up here, but Jane apparently didn't take it seriously enough. Since arriving at Base Camp though, she's been noticeably bothered by the altitude, and we've been spared her restless, quicksilver energy and torrents of speech. Now she shows up for meals, if she participates at all, attired in four water bottles and an over-sized down jacket. I believe she's looking forward to getting the hell out of here in a couple of days.

O

Climbing Plan For
Sagarmatha Environmental Expedition 1996

APRIL

9	*Puja* ceremony at Base Camp (~17,600 ft/5,364 m)
10	First attempt through Khumbu Icefall
11	Base Camp to Icefall (turn-around time: noon)
	Return to Base Camp
12	Base Camp
13–15	Icefall. One night at Camp I (~19,500 ft/5,943 m)
	Return to Base Camp for rest
16–20	Base Camp to Camp II (~21,300 ft/6,492 m)
	One night at Camp I
	One night at Camp II
	Proceed to the base of Lhotse Face
	Return to Base Camp
21–22	Rest at Base Camp
23–26	Base Camp to Camp II
	One night at Camp II
	Climb Lhotse Face to Camp III (~24,000 ft/7,315 m)
	First night at Camp III
	Return to Camp II
	One night at Camp II
	Return to Base Camp
27–30	Rest at Base Camp, or further down at Gorak Shep, Lobuche or Ama Dablam Garden Lodge on Anatoli's recommendation

MAY

1–2	Rest at Base Camp or further down
3	Base Camp to Camp II
4	Rest day at Camp II
5	Camp II to Camp III

6   Camp III to South Col (~26,000 ft/7,925 m)
7–8   South Col to the summit (29,028 ft/8,848 m/~5.5 miles
             above sea level)

Scott and Anatoli exhaustively discuss the climbing itinerary. There
are several ways to summit Everest, and a climber's preference is determined by his or her personality and the experiences the climber
has had on the mountain.

Anatoli swears by a truly rigorous method: During each ascent we
must press ourselves to the utmost and then one step further—climb
a notch higher, shovel more snow, move more ice blocks. He realizes
that it's hard, and that it hurts—you must have the will to suffer. Then
we must descend as far as possible and alternate between rest and
activity. The body and psyche will acclimatize in this intermediate
period, and we will be in better shape the next time we ascend.

Anatoli also believes it's best to take a long rest period before the summit bid. Each time we are up high, our bodies get extremely debilitated and drained of strength, even if we think we're doing better
"upstairs." The human organism cannot regenerate at altitude, so it's
crucial to pull oneself together, leave Base Camp and trek downwards,
though that means a long trek back before the summit attempt.
Anatoli's plan is to descend as far as Ama Dablam Garden Lodge,
where he'll be surrounded by the flowering rhododendron forest, bird
songs (romantic!) and, Martin comments, women. If I move my bulk
that far away from Base Camp, I'm afraid I won't have the energy to
return and climb!

Scott's considering a faster schedule, but I predict he'll not be capable
of pushing himself as fast as he thinks. And, just looking at folks'
problems now and visualizing how our health will deteriorate even
more as we climb higher, there is no way the rest of us will make it! I

also know that Scott elegantly, flexibly, adapts to reality. He's in complete agreement with an extended rest period before the summit bid, but dreads the possibility of stomach infections if we descend to the villages below Base Camp.

Neal is leaning toward Scott's plan, but after supper, when the expedition members express their impression that there's plenty of time and that they'd prefer to acclimatize properly, he and Scott seem more inclined toward Anatoli's way of thinking.

I listen and learn. I've never climbed an 8,000-meter peak, so I have to learn from those who have. Along the way I'll form my own opinion—when I've been there. But I'm inclined toward Anatoli's plan. I know I can't go on and on without breaks. But with the correct balance of rest and work, I can achieve nearly anything—over a time span.

APRIL 9, 1996

Beautiful day! Huge ceremony. The biggest I've participated in. The Sherpas have truly lavished great care on the details and I shoot picture after picture. Neal is on my back again, acting like a school teacher. Who cares? I prefer Scott as a photography teacher.

Lopsang and his fellow Sherpas have completed the camp altar. I'm in awe of their ability to build with the available stone, but of course their survival has been dependent on this skill. Lopsang's twenty-three-foot-long bamboo pole is erected in the center of the altar, and from it, row upon row of prayer flags are being pulled out over our entire camp. Pemba and Krishna run one of the prayer-flag lines over the top of my tent and anchor it with big rocks on the far side. What an exquisite privilege to have prayer flags flying above my home. May a few of the blessing prayers fall on me before the wind carries them to the heavens. *Om mani padme hum.*

The bamboo pole and lines of prayer flags must present quite a sight for the trekkers passing by. When we were in Pakistan, Lopsang initiated the puja ceremony with recitations of Buddhist scriptures, but now older men are present and the honorable task is allotted to them.

Until the puja has been performed, none of our expedition members can set foot on the notorious Khumbu Icefall, the gateway to Mount Everest. That would be an unforgivable violation of the Gods and would stir bad fortune.

The puja must be performed on a specific day, decided by the most prominent lama in Khumbu, supposedly after he's consulted the sun, moon and stars. Initially the word is that the puja can't take place until Friday, but then it's decided that it will be held today, Tuesday, which sparks the dry comment from Sandy, "It's unbelievable how you can influence the Gods by using the right payment."

Who knows?

Haze and fragrance from the lit incense hang above the altar. Quite an assembly: eleven expedition members and the invaluable Sherpas— kitchen and high-altitude staff, local yak drivers, porters and those from other expeditions who have accepted our invitation of "All are welcome!"

Anatoli's "private doctor" is present. Linda Wylie is a fascinating woman from Santa Fe, New Mexico. Every afternoon she comes tiptoeing, moving like a graceful gazelle from Henry Todd's camp, where she lives, to Anatoli's tent, where she sleeps. Unnoticed by most, she slips into the flowery tent. Every time the wind blows from the Icefall, it carries Anatoli's voice and guitar to my ears. Every morning and every night, he plays the wistful songs of his beloved home country to his heart's content. Anatoli's singing makes me long for simplicity, depth, fullness . . . belonging.

Three Sherpas recite from the oblong scripture books. Though I don't understand the actual words, I nonetheless come under the spell of the solemn ambiance. The rice-throwing ritual is about to begin. Rice is distributed, and when the Sherpas throw it into the air, we follow their example.

After half an hour the solemnity is over, and the fun starts. Chang, the milky Nepalese rice booze, is distributed extravagantly, followed by Kukri rum. Most important now is tying the lama-blessed red bands around our necks. They will protect us against all evil and bring us back safely from our risky journey. I ask Lopsang to tie mine. Consecrated white silk scarves follow.

The kitchen staff serves tiny butter sculptures. And then we must consume something that looks—and tastes—like shit, but swallowed with plenty of beer and grimaces, it merely steps up the festive atmosphere. Offerings from our abundant supply of goodies are broken out and shared.

The revelry nearly makes us forget about the ice axes. But not really, because though we party now, the serious purpose behind the celebration lurks. We begin tomorrow! So we fetch our ice axes. I've got five. Two for mixed rock, ice and snow, two special ice axes and a super-lightweight axe for summit day that's good for nothing but stopping me—I hope—in case of an accidental fall.

All axes are on the altar, being blessed, and will remain in the care of the Gods overnight. First thing in the morning, before dawn's break, we'll pick them up on our way to the Icefall.

Kim Sejberg from the International Commercial expedition comes visiting. Nice. See Michael Jørgensen later on; he's visiting Anatoli and, for a tiny bit, me. Good company. I want to summit Mount Everest—and safely return! No O_2! Be strong and preferably graceful. I want to participate in the expeditions that will inevitably follow on the international climbing scene after this "stunt." I'm satisfyingly installed in my little tent home, and prayer flags embellish my garden. I consider it a special blessing and gift. Feeling competent, collected, balanced: trusting myself. I am strong! I wish only the best for my teammates and me.

Before I turn in, I prepare my climbing harness with the necessary slings with jumar and screw carabiners, figure-eight descender for rappeling, extra carabiners and prusik lines in case of emergency. My plastic boots stand ready, crampons adjusted. Repair kit in my backpack. The longest ice axe will be strapped to the outside of the pack; PowerBars and spare gloves go inside. And, not forgotten, the coin Johnny gave me the morning of my departure. The three musketeers—Steff, Johnny and I—joined efforts to create the drug treatment center, King's Island. I realize how much this coin meant to him—so it does to me. This first ascent is with as light a load as possible. Next time, a full load.

The morning schedule looks like this:

4:30	Wake-up tea
5:00	Breakfast
5:30	Departure

Today's goal is to climb as far as possible through the Icefall. Turn-around time is noon, whether we are through or not. As we acclimatize and improve our form, we'll need less time to climb to the end of the Icefall. In the Icefall, especially, speed and safety are inextricably linked. As soon as the sun gets high enough to warm the ice, shit starts to happen up there. Not that this strategy provides a guarantee nothing will fall on our heads before then, as the Khumbu Glacier moves several feet every day.

Ages back, I asked Scott, "How long do you estimate it'll take me to climb the Icefall the first time?"

"For you, my dear, nine hours. For me, five and a half. Later we'll speed up."

Lying in my sleeping bag, I send prayers into the pitch-dark night that we'll all return safely from our first venture through the Icefall tomorrow.

Khumbu Icefall

APRIL 10, 1996
I absolutely detest getting up early in the morning—that's one point where I'm a lousy climber! This morning I am one of the last in the mess tent. I drink plenty of fluids but can't eat the chapati or omelette. At this ungodly hour my stomach declines food. Skip the vitamin circus as well; don't have the courage to gulp down fifteen to twenty capsules before an intense physical challenge combined, in a killing cocktail, with altitude!

Pete, Klev and Dale are long gone. Sandy and Martin are leaving the mess tent as I arrive. Scott and Neal will take the "sweep" position and go last. Tim and Charlotte are waiting for me. Lene, how the hell can you be so slow, I berate myself. Fill the flask, water and Gatorade. Anatoli won't start to think about climbing until a couple of hours after we've left, most likely.

Off we go, passing through a society of Base Camp denizens, half dozing. We're starting out a little early, so no other teams are heading our way yet. Greet David Breashears, leader of the IMAX expedition. David is filming a multimillion-dollar documentary about climbing Everest. Seems like a decent guy; he and Sandy have undertaken several projects together.

Get your ass in gear, Lene. It's now or never, I tell myself as I fall in behind Charlotte and Tim. Our dear Doctor Ingrid has gotten out of her sleeping bag, just to see us off properly at the entrance to the Icefall. The front-runners are waiting for us at the flat spot where people usually put on their crampons. First trip through the Icefall, we'll suffer together. Feels safe. Headlamps are no longer needed; it's becoming light.

O

I'm here!

At the start of the actual climb. I've been working like a dog for so long to be able to be here today. I'm excited—not nervous or frightened. I have consciously chosen to face and accept the conditions that rule here; therefore, fear is unnecessary.

The Icefall is magnificent. The first time I saw it, back in 1991, I thought of Niagara Falls—instantly frozen. Our route takes us directly through this abundance of blue ice, greenish ice, snowy ice. I tail the others, and we begin our ascent. It's strenuous. Altitude and the gradient make themselves felt!

First ladder crossing. I've studied pictures and listened to stories about the aluminium ladders used for crossing crevasses in the Khumbu Icefall. It can sometimes take more than three or four ladders lashed together to span an abyss. All you have to do is walk straight across. Right!

I watch Scott and listen. "Step on every second step, use the fixed ropes as railing and your body's weight for balancing." Okay! Bless my years of balance training. Certain I can cross these ladders in elegant style, I focus my eyes at a point on the far side, step on every second step and I'm over. My teammates are impressed.

Charlotte performs a variation. She detests ladders, and we must use seventy-seven of them to climb the Icefall. "I have nothing against the Khumbu Icefall," she says with sly wit. "I just hate the way you have to get through it!" But nothing stops this woman, so she's down on her butt worming herself across. Method tested and successful. Later it comes out that Pete often takes advantage of the same technique, but only when no ladies are in sight!

Going up and around ice formations, crossing crevasses, scaling ladders, carefully placing my crampons, balancing, clipping my carabiner to the fixed ropes. Should I take a fall, there's a fair chance the ropes will break the descent, but I have no desire to test whether these life insurance lines will work, so I gather my concentration instead. No picture-taking today. Each thing at its appropriate time, and just one priority counts now: Up! God! This is harsh work! Panting and puffing, I envy Scott, who shoots up the Icefall. Ha, ha—touché! Since he discovered the mountains as a fourteen-year-old, he hasn't done much else. How great to watch him thrive—here in his true element.

Martin's coughing like a madman. The Khumbu Cough.

Hour after hour our team slogs its way upwards. Holy smoke. Are we never stopping for a break? Though in the Icefall, there is no decidedly safe spot to rest. But I'm not going to be the wimp, so I drag myself up. Hard work. Guess I have to leave the blessed and merciful realm of laziness behind and get a grip on Anatoli's "will to suffer." As a matter of fact, my life project before committing to Everest was to *reduce* my suffering. I trusted that I'd suffered sufficiently already.

Spot Scott sitting at the top of a ladder. Clip my carabiner on the rope, grab with both hands, and direct my boots meticulously upwards, step by step. Crampons and the struggle to breathe don't make this any easier. Have to be certain the boot hits the middle of the step, between two rows of crampon points.

Dump myself down, puffing, next to Scott. "You are doing good," he says. If he had the faintest clue how hard I strive to give that impression. After a slow morning, my competitive mentality has put me in the front. Pretend innocence, but satisfied inside. That's why I'm here. To perform well.

"So are you, Scott. You are strong," is my reply. And I'm happy, too, that he is.

O

Christ, how much longer can this go on? Must change my mental attitude, stop tormenting myself by asking that kind of superfluous question. How far? A mile and a quarter, mile and a half direct rise in approximately one month's time—beat that! So the brain must be tuned to infinite and in "enjoy the ride" mode.

Onward. Upward. Ascending. A few glimpses to lure one up the route to the Western Cwm. And a few delightful glances at the huge rock faces on either side with their enormous beauty. But mainly hard, relentless work. Lack of O_2 sure takes its toll.

We head to our right, toward the Nuptse Wall, ascending a long, exposed snow ridge, up, then down, climbing ladders and blue ice. Through a field of the hardest glacier ice, like green and blue crystal. More crevasses, more ladders, an ice wall. Using the fixed ropes as much as possible: Grab it high and haul myself upwards, stemming with my thigh muscles. No style, solemnly economizing power. Ice axe proves itself to be more in the way than helpful. Strange style of mountaineering!

Pass the Taiwanese expedition. Rumor has it it's a highly unprofessional group; here they are moving slowly. Left again, following a narrow ice spur with a sheer drop on our left and sheer rise on our right. Will it tumble over us later?

Up, down, up, across, around, then suddenly I face a 150-foot-tall icy wall, a challenge that reminds me of genuine climbing, supported though by ladders and fixed ropes. Jumar clipped on the rope, I push it upward bit by bit, taking breaks to catch my breath—just barely. More climbers behind me; this passage will create a bottleneck, as climbers queue up to ascend and descend. Trying to memorize the route, imprint it in my brain. Want to be prepared if I, because of some crisis, have to get through this at night or in bad weather.

Sun's beginning to gain power, and in what seems like a second, this deep freezer is transformed into desert-beating heat. Off with the Gore-Tex jacket. On with the sun block and glacier goggles. Not the time or the place to become snow-blind or sunburned. Nausea, *fuck!* It's tough, pretending it's not. If you can't make it, fake it—takes you anywhere. If I think this is too hard, how the hell can I aim for the summit? Yeah, I'm only inquiring, Lene Gammelgaard. So I continue—naturally—sweat pouring down me.

Aha! The Mousetrap. I see why Kim Sejberg referred to it with awe in his voice. A massive leaning tower of ice, which looms above us at a frightening angle. Unfortunately the only way past the Mousetrap is to climb up and over it. I look at the serac apprehensively. It will fall—the only question is when? Only one option: *Go!*—with ice in my stomach—and no stopping. Almost through this overhanging nightmare, one crampon comes loose as I hammer the front points into the ice to climb the remaining vertical feet. "Come on!" Scott's yelling. "This is not the place to take a break."

One final snow wall to climb, this one more alpinelike with jumar and crampon technique. Hard work! Carabiner unlocked from one rope, clipped on to the next, following a snow ridge curving slightly around to the left.

Suddenly I am at the end, the Western Cwm's breathtaking beauty unfolding before me. I'm spinning, spinning, around and around . . . Everest, Lhotse, Nuptse—three massive cliffs—each one incredible, together, overwhelming. Pumori is behind me, the Western Cwm's high plateau of permanent ice and snow ahead. Panting, gasping for breath, tears streaming down my face, I break down in awe, crying with overwhelming joy.

I've come home. This sight outweighs all the hardships I've gone through to get here.

Though I am the first Danish—Scandinavian—woman to set foot here, I couldn't care less at the moment. What's important is experiencing this fairy-tale landscape, no matter how many or how few have trodden here before—and so it should be on any mountain.

Moving on, I come to Pete, Klev, Dale and Scott sitting on the mushroom-shaped pinnacle of an ice tower between abysses. I literally throw myself on top of them, touching everyone, a hug here, a kiss there, seeing they know what it's about. Scott receives a giant hug: "Thank you for giving me this opportunity. I am deeply grateful." "I knew you would understand," Scott answers. Yeah. We need to share the most precious things in life with people we value highly and who understand.

After we've consumed our Gatorade, nuts and PowerBars, Pete, Klev and Dale begin the descent to Base Camp. Scott continues up accompanied by Neal and Anatoli, who have caught up with us. Charlotte, Tim, Martin and I start up the Western Cwm together. But the urgency has evaporated; I'm in no hurry. I settle myself on the backpack and let everything sink in: I tackled the notorious Icefall in fewer than five hours! I'm strong enough. Doing splendidly on the technical skills. And I am here among the highest mountains in the world. Here, where my heart feels at home. In place. I am fulfilled. I am simply happy.

Sandy comes, and we start out toward our Camp I, which is higher than the usual Camp I area. Anatoli insists on that site, and the Sherpas support his arguments. We are better sheltered there from avalanches and in the long run, it will make our access to Camp II easier. But, for the moment, it's too far for me as well as for Sandy. I feel the effects of too little oxygen and realize it's turn-around time for me.

Still, I have achieved more than I dared hope.

Base Camp

APRIL 11, 1996
Rest day. Anatoli's singing. I am drawn in by the melody. Anatoli engages me. His entire being. "I am a Kazakh man." Modest and yet not. He knows his own worth.

Sun rays strike my tent, and I watch as the prayer flags' shadows caress the tent. My emergency toilet lies behind the big rock the prayer flag line is attached to, and I take much delight in the flags every time nature calls during the night. Promised Flemming I'd bring some home.

Met Henrik Jessen Hansen and Bo Belvedere at their camp yesterday, a pleasant visit.

I'll try to get hold of my father and mother later on today. Our time, 11 A.M.—their time, in Denmark, 5 P.M. I've been thinking it over, whether they would prefer to shut their eyes to the whole business until I'm safely home (hopefully), whether my calls will only increase the pain and terror I cause them by coming here? Arrived at the conclusion that I can call and ask them. Borrowing Sandy's equipment will make it realistic to call once a week, if they'd like me to. At the very least, weekly contact may remove the anxiety caused by not knowing.

My parents were the last to know of my decision to climb Everest. I postponed telling them about it as long as possible, but a media campaign was planned for November 27, and I didn't want them to learn of my plans from the newspapers. I am well aware of how devastating it is to sit powerless, waiting, while a loved one is out "having a ball." I knew that once they were informed they wouldn't be capable of truly relaxing until they saw me again, meaning a minimum of five months. So I stalled and stalled . . . until the day my brother's wife, Vibeke, called.

"Lene, we had dinner with your parents last night, and Claus slipped and revealed that you're going to Everest!"

"Vibeke, where is Claus? That's the best news I've received in a long time."

I phoned my beloved big brother and thanked him deeply for that slip of his tongue. Now that the bomb had been set off, I could relate honestly to my parents again. This had been my greatest predicament in relation to Project Everest: wanting to protect my loved ones from pain and, at the same time, wanting to pursue the summit. I am aware that should I choose to continue climbing high mountains, it might have heavy emotional consequences. A person acquainted with life and death may have difficulty maintaining a close emotional connection to someone like me. I know, because I am not capable, myself, of maintaining a tight bond with a person who risks dying every time he or she goes climbing, and who apparently gives higher priority to climbing mountains than to intimacy and the obligations it entails. To how much pain can you expose the people you care about, before they give up emotionally? I suppose you could choose to create an emotional life in the society of international climbers and fulfill the basic human needs among them. And that's a grand lifestyle!

One of the reasons I respect Anatoli is his sense of reality. He is a mountaineer, and yes, he's after the fourteen peaks higher than 8,000 meters, but he knows he risks dying out here and, therefore, has not started a family.

I respect this either/or philosophy and understand it more than the attitude of those climbers who want it all, who choose to have a family and then spend more months away from their families than with them. It's one thing if the partner fully accepts those terms and can live with the risks. It's another matter if the partner suffers each time the climber takes off anew to challenge fate. I don't feel sorry for them, however; they have a choice. In turn, I realize people may choose not to be involved with me for the same reasons.

During my preparations for Everest, I withdrew emotionally from close relationships. Partly I was in desperate need of all my energy to get the "business" up and running. But I'm guessing this emotional withdrawal was also necessary to risk what I'm now in the middle of.

I've found myself thinking, "If human relationships are not more satisfying and fulfilling than this, I might as well scale mountains and live the adventurous side of life," knowing full well that fulfillment is dependent on the degree to which I invest in others. But it seems that the more emotionally involved I become, the less I'm able to follow my own desires.

○

Called my parents using the satellite phone. A really good idea. Funny—sitting in the middle of absolutely nowhere, press a Danish telephone number and . . .

Ring . . . Ring . . .

"*Det er Helge*," my father answers, so clearly it seems as if he's across the street.

"It's your daughter calling from Base Camp. Been up and down the Icefall one time, and I am safe and in great shape."

It demands more courage to be totally honest with them about what I'm doing than it takes to climb Everest. Just can't possibly imagine how bizarre it must be, being parents to someone like me. I just pray my kids will never expose me to such. But I know my father well enough to intuit that he's touched and glad I called.

"Read your first article in *Ekstra Bladet* last Sunday. Vibeke brought it. Very well written."

Good feeling to hear the article has been printed. Beginning to see a flicker of the scope of this enterprise.

They want me to phone every week.

O

Throwing a party tonight for Sandy's fortieth birthday. She's expressed gratitude that I waited for her in the Icefall yesterday. She was exhausted and, therefore, despairing. I know the feeling, so I slowed my pace to hers. I know I can help people perform their best by not focusing or commenting on their weakness but merely leading the way. Usually they discover they are capable of a lot more than they thought they were. That way they overcome any obstacle—with dignity intact. She told me she hadn't expected another woman to be supportive: "Maybe there's a difference between American and Scandinavian female climbers," she commented. "American women are extremely competitive and would never have let themselves be detained by me."

Could that be just how you perceive the world and exist in it, Sandy? I wonder. The climber in me knows, though, that she hasn't worked thoroughly enough on the fundamental attitude: "You are 100 percent responsible for yourself. You must not expect anybody to help you." Sandy ought to be tougher than this, considering her climbing history.

APRIL 13, 1996
Second time through the Icefall after spending the night at Camp I at 19,500 feet. No problem! Timed myself on the distance from Camp I and down—one and a half hours! I'm content. Our team, except Tim, Klev, Pete and me, used the day to climb the slope of the Western

Cwm where Camp II will be. Pressing the limits of their performing ability. I wanted to go down to rest and feel good about that decision. I'm still going for no O_2.

Need to write an article for *Ekstra Bladet* tomorrow. Feeling strong and independent.

O

Linda, Anatoli's friend, accepted our dinner invitation. She was an authentic boon to our social gathering—a beautiful soul. Anatoli's calling me Jeanne d'Arc. That's something. And David Breashears says he saw me in the Icefall. *Strong!* I'll climb this mountain.

Linda recommends that I team up with Brigitte, a strong New Zealand woman who wants to summit Everest and has bought a space on Henry Todd's expedition. She's committed and experienced.

APRIL 15, 1996

Quickly recovering from the reprimand I received because I decided to come down to Base Camp from Camp I yesterday instead of ascending for acclimatization. But I "ran" down to train for speed at altitude. I trust my assessment of the situation. Taking my cold sores and snotty nose into account, I pushed myself to the utmost. But lack of trust from others threatens to undermine my motivation, to set fire to my old "I'll show you" program, which I hate, because it makes me lose focus.

And I can see that the ones who are pushing on, regardless . . . Scott, Sandy, Neal and Martin . . . are all feeling sick and taking altitude medicine. It doesn't make sense.

Ingrid and Tim are out of here—both going down to a lower altitude because of AMS symptoms. This morning at breakfast, Ingrid sat there down in the mouth, totally unlike her. I asked her how she was feeling and instinctively gave her a huge hug. She started crying. She's having a hell of a time dealing with the altitude; since Lobuche, she had been on Diamox, which helped her acclimatize, but she stopped taking it to see if her body could do the job itself. With bad results. She wants to be competent and dependable, and she truly is! But she has underestimated the effects of altitude.

Charlotte and Sandy join in, and we hold an impromptu girl-comforting session to make Ingrid feel better about having to make the only possible decision. "Go down! Stay down till you have recovered, and then come back up," we tell her. It turns out that she had been on her way down this morning, but got lost on the glacier.

"Tim's not well," Charlotte says. "I'll ask if he wants to go down with you. This will be pretty tricky though, cause he gives me the silent treatment if I ask how he's doing."

Scott comes in—looks at us a bit with a questioning gaze. Afterwards he asks me what's going on and wonders aloud why Ingrid didn't come to him with her problems.

O

Scott's fallen ill again. I must try to transform my frustration into goal-focused energy.

6:05 P.M. It's freezing—I'm demoralized.

Scott has now adjusted our climbing itinerary to match reality. Good!

APRIL 16, 1996
Delivered article number two and eleven rolls of film for transport to *Ekstra Bladet*.

It's snowing!

I am prepared for climbing.

O

Cozy afternoon in the mess tent in the company of Anatoli, Scott, Sandy, Jane and the American consul David Schensted, who is out here trekking and "nurturing" national interests. Quite a bunch of celebrities from the States gathered here.

I'm often asked if I'm not bored stiff being in Base Camp for so many days. But so much is going on here: Trekkers come visiting every day; I pop in at some other camp; or intriguing personalities drop in at our place, grabbing a mug of Starbucks and some splendid company. The Mountain Madness camp is *it*, the spot where people most want to pass some time, because they feel welcome—and they are!

I adore this lifestyle. If love were here, it would be my version of Paradise. Hmmm—what a fine evening.

I'm ready for the Icefall tomorrow!

Camp II

APRIL 19, 1996
After three rounds of the Icefall, one night at Camp I and another night at Camp II—with a spurt to the Lhotse Face and a speed

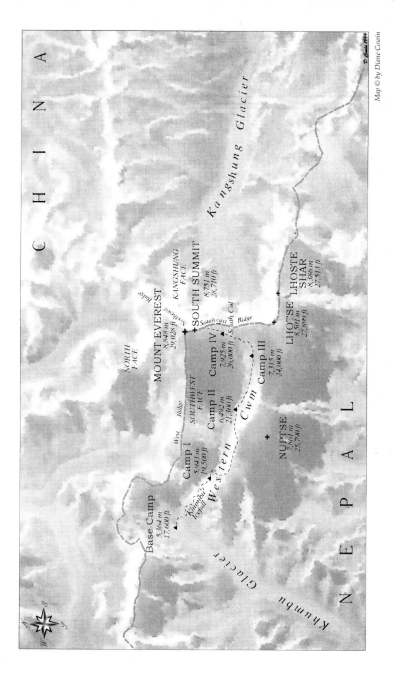

C H I N A

Kangshung Glacier

Northeast Ridge

MOUNT EVEREST
8,848 m
29,028 ft

KANGSHUNG
FACE

SOUTH SUMMIT
8,751 m
28,710 ft

NORTH
FACE

Southeast Ridge

South Col

LHOTSE
8,501 m
27,890 ft

LHOTSE
SHAR
8,386 m
27,513 ft

SOUTHWEST
FACE

Camp IV
7,925 m
26,000 ft

West Ridge

Camp II
6,492 m
21,300 ft

Camp III
7,315 m
24,000 ft

Camp I
5,943 m
19,500 ft

Western Cwm

Khumbu
Icefall

NUPTSE
7,861 m
25,790 ft

Base Camp
5,364 m
17,600 ft

Khumbu Glacier

N E P A L

N
W   E
S

Map © by Diane Coavin

D. Coavin 1999

Sagarmatha environmental expedition team, 1996

Base Camp

Our route

Buddhist chorten, memorial to
Tenzing Norgay, Namche

Kathmandu

Scott Fischer and Lene Gammelgaard

Base Camp

Anatoli's tent

Anatoli Boukreev and Lene Gammelgaard

Prayer flags at Base Camp

The puja ceremony, Base Camp

Gyalzen preparing for the puja

Khumbu Icefall

Lene Gammelgaard (above) and Scott Fisher (below) climbing the Icefall

Ladders roped together

Camp I

Team members crossing a crevasse

Climbers on the route to Camp II

Lene Gammelgaard and Sandy Pittman at Camp II

Climbers at the Yellow Band

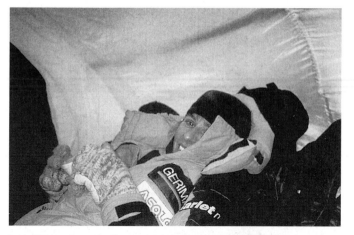

Lene Gammelgaard in her tent at Camp IV

Camp IV with oxygen tanks

Climbers on the Hillary Step

Lene Gammelgaard on the summit

View at 8300 meters

South Col with huddle site (left) and Camp IV tents (right)

Lene Gammelgaard, after the storm

Lopsang returns to Camp II

Memorial service, Base Camp

Lene Gammelgaard, back in Kathmandu

descent—I feel in good shape. Scott's at Base Camp. Illness made him pull back and relax a bit. Ingrid and Tim are back. Tim's got the most engaging, warm smile, and it feels wonderful to be enriched by it again. Ingrid is at least one experience richer. She takes it easier, is seemingly milder. Humbled?

David, the American consul, told us that he had found Ingrid, staggering, in Gorak Shep. She had fallen into his arms, saying: "I need help. I must get into a Gamow bag." Ingrid got the medical care she needed at the high-altitude clinic at Pheriche. It's reassuring, having a doctor go through the treatment she gives to others.

So many people on this peak. When I first committed to scaling Everest and began searching for information about our route, I found it hard to come to terms with the fact that I was participating in a commercial expedition and that Everest is no longer pristine. Perhaps as many as two hundred people, from all over the globe, occupy Base Camp. An entire society pops up overnight twice a year when it's summiting season.

Preferably, I would arrange my own expedition, on my terms, but that would take me years! And the experience I can gain by climbing on Scott's team is worth a few compromises.

Normally, when I seek out the wilderness, I'm escaping—trying to avoid big groups of people. But Everest is not as it was when Edmund Hillary and others explored these regions. Gradually I've adjusted to the reality that rules climbing the "big 8's" in our decade and, now, I wouldn't like it any different. It's inspiring being part of this society, encountering great personalities truly worth listening to. I have a fascinating talk with a guy from Alaska who has lived his entire life doing what one would call "men's work"—working on oil platforms, mining, hunting, you name it. In my little corner of the world atlas, there aren't many men left who do what men used to do. Interesting!

Base Camp

APRIL 20, 1996

Thinking about summiting without using supplemental oxygen and how to take the best possible care of my sponsors. Must shoot sponsor pics today. Music floating my way from the mess tent. I'm home. Happy.

APRIL 21, 1996

Scott's ascending with Pete to Camp I. Pete's still having trouble sleeping at altitude; he had to descend last time. Klev hasn't left his side, but now Scott's going up with Pete to help him acclimatize. They are both one cycle behind, Pete because of the sleeping disturbance, Scott because of illness.

I want Everest: summit—safe return—no O_2.

Breakfast and draft of climbing plan. Anatoli hands me a butterfly. "That's you at South Col," he says. The butterfly barely moves, it's either dead or torpid because of the cold. I look for a safe spot on a warm rock for it. Maybe the sun will bring it back to life.

Scott rebuked this proud man yesterday while I was present. Tactless! Anatoli had just returned from the mountain, after having put in more fixed ropes on the route between Camps II and III, the most demanding and dangerous job on an expedition—he's a hard-working guy who demands everything of himself, but little from his surroundings.

Scott and I were sharing a cozy afternoon, sipping beer, taking pictures of each other in front of the Icefall with various sponsors' gadgets.

I left, discreetly, when Scott started in on Anatoli.

"Anatoli, you were hired to guide on this trip—to mingle with the team—not just to work hard high on the mountain. If you merely function as a strong climber, I might as well have hired an altitude Sherpa."

Anatoli was silent.

"I had to pull rank on him," Scott apologized afterward. "People have been complaining that he doesn't socialize."

It's unusual for Scott to address people in that manner. Normally he doesn't get angry or disrespectful. Was it Sandy, lately "best buddies" with Scott, who complained? I've heard her grumble about Anatoli. I've defended him and tried to talk her into taking the initiative and getting to know him better.

"He's a proud man, Scott. I don't know how he will react to this."

Ambiance destroyed. I know who *I* trust the most.

Anatoli did show up for dinner last night. Thank God. But, of course, having grown up in the Soviet Union, he's survived worse than a childish American boss. When I told him I was sorry that I happened to overhear the rebuke, and that it was undeserved and disgraceful, his only response was, "It has actually no significance."

I trust he's much bigger than that—capable of seeing through Scott's words—finding the right attitude. I think the butterfly is a sign he's okay.

O

Bathing in our small blue shower tent created from the last piece of tarpaulin, accompanied by Anatoli's songs and guitar.

O

Scott radios that he and Pete are at Camp II. Splendid news. They'll come down tomorrow. I'll go up again the day after tomorrow. Camp II, Camp III, Camp IV—the ultimate preparations for the summit bid. I am 100 percent committed.

Brent Bishop arrived yesterday. Nice guy. Brent's the coordinator of the expedition's environmental project; he summited Everest in 1994 with Scott and Lopsang.

Brent is gasping a bit. "Took six days to get here from Kathmandu. I'm acclimatizing pretty fast, and now I'm assisting in the cleanup of an old dumpsite on the outskirts of Base Camp. I guess it's about ten years old and was exposed recently as the glacier tossed and turned."

Brent is amazed at the means of communication available here: "I was here in '94, and we had no way to communicate other than by mail runners. Out of the fourteen teams I've counted here at Base Camp, at least half have brought satellite phones. Pretty strange to be hiking around on the opposite side of the globe, and then have messages from my wife waiting for me when I arrive in the middle of nowhere!"

The cleanup has practically become an industry—totally under control and functioning smoothly, apart from Lopsang's trying to wangle a sky-high price for carrying the huge five-liter oxygen containers down from the South Col.

O

Funny evening with crazy people in our mess tent. A friend of Brent's, Steve, ate dinner with us. He's going for Lhotse—snowboarding down! Handsome fellow. Ranks among the toughest snowboarders in the world and apparently lives by the maxim "Live fast, die young, and leave a handsome corpse." Compared to his plan, climbing Everest sounds like a picnic. Martin baptizes him "Plankman."

I try to watch the American movie *Cliffhanger* on Sandy's disc TV. "No way! A harness could never break like that. Wow! Climbing ice in a T-shirt—no ice axes." The film is a farce if you are acquainted with climbing in real life. Watching videos at Base Camp is too much for me, and I leave, even though the Sherpas' absorption in the movie is almost worth staying for.

APRIL 22, 1996

Phoned my parents. Good! Wrote expedition postcards. Slight nausea. I will not put up with obstacles to my summiting. I ignore it.

One of our Sherpas, Ngawang Topche Sherpa, is seriously ill up at Camp II. Scott and Pete are on their way down—somewhere between Camp II, which they left this morning, and Base Camp—so they're not aware of the drama taking place higher up. Klev and Tim are at Camp II and, seemingly, have the situation under control, as much as you can have pulmonary edema under control. Precise, calm reports come over the walkie-talkies to Ingrid: pulse, treatment and the general state of the Sherpa. I'm impressed by their ability to handle a critical situation. Charlotte is well acquainted with Tim's emergency medical treatment skills: "He's used to scenarios like this; after all, that's what he does for a living back home," she assures us. I remember that Tim works professionally as a ski patroller in Colorado.

"Sounds as if he's about to drown in his own lung fluids," Klev's deliberate voice recounts over the air.*

Ingrid poses a line of questions. They try the Gamow bag in combination with medication. Nothing seems to help. The entire Camp II village has been alerted and is planning how to get Ngawang down as fast as possible. That means going through the Icefall after dusk.

O

I'm set and packed for tomorrow, the last ascent before the actual summit bid. Preparing myself for tough work, discomfort and brand new challenges on the mountain for the coming four to six days and nights. My pack is heavy: camera, tripod, freeze-dried Nasi Goreng, raisin-nut cocktail, extra woolen underwear to leave at Camp III for the summit bid, the obligatory water flask, an extra pair of goggles, silk sleeping bag liner for warmth and, of course, my pocket pharmacy, including an emergency survival kit in case I or someone near me is hit by the effects of high altitude.

At Camp II, they're struggling to keep Ngawang in the Gamow bag, but he's scared of it and doesn't comprehend their instructions, so they give bottled oxygen a try. If he's not seriously affected, Ngawang ought to recover relatively fast, but to prevent a relapse, he must have oxygen for the next six to twelve hours. No matter what, he has to come down—as soon as possible.

---

* High-altitude pulmonary edema (HAPE) typically develops from acute mountain sickness (AMS). The lungs fill with fluids that block oxygen transfer to the blood, and the drop in the concentration of oxygen in the blood leads to impaired brain function and a telltale blue face. Early symptons can include coughing, shortness of breath, a feeling of suffocation at night, weakness and fatigue. Because of the lack of oxygen, symptoms of AMS—headache, lack of appetite, nausea, vomiting—get more severe. Confusion, delirium and irrational behavior indicate significant oxygen deprivation in the brain. If the person falls into a coma, death may occur in six to twelve hours unless the victim receives a concentration of oxygen, either bottled or pumped into a Gamow bag, and is brought down to a lower altitude.

Lopsang doesn't seem to grasp the profound seriousness of the situation: "But he's just coughing. He's Sherpa; he is strong. I have the same cough." It's beginning to dawn on us that Sherpas do not know or acknowledge altitude sickness in the form of pulmonary edema. Being dependent on their strength for survival, they seem to find it difficult to accept something that, to them, implies weakness: Sherpas by definition cannot become altitude sick. To them, altitude affects only non-Sherpas.

I introduce Ingrid and Neal to Henrik Jessen Hansen and Jan Mathorne at Malcolm "Mal" Duff's camp, another Scottish expedition. Henrik is a skilled altitude doctor, and Ingrid consults him concerning Ngawang's case.

Jan Mathorne has become a father since I last saw him. I must hear how that is and check up on the latest helicopter rescues. When you hear a helicopter, it almost always means yet another climber has been injured. The first this season was a Sherpa who fell into a hidden crevasse in the Western Cwm. Next was a young guy from Mal Duff's team, a British marine and super-athlete in his late twenties, who suffered a heart attack between Camps I and II. "Not necessarily a consequence of altitude, but there might be a connection," says Henrik. Ingrid hurries on to Rob Hall's camp for additional assistance for Ngawang.

Scott and Pete are down safely. They entered camp with broad grins on their faces after spending a grand day in each other's company, only to be confronted with the drama that's taking place in the camp they left six hours ago.

Neal's preparing to head up into the Icefall before it gets dark. Klev and Tim are bringing Ngawang down to Camp I, where Neal will take over, guiding the eight-man rescue mission through the Icefall.

This is serious.

It's snowing! Just hope it won't interfere with the rescue and our ascent in the morning.

Base Camp to Camp II

APRIL 23, 1996

I started out on this, my fourth trip through the Icefall, at a time when I knew I would have it almost to myself. I want to find out where I'm at, as far as conditioning goes. Last time I was like a snake in first gear, slow, slow. Even Anatoli started nagging me. But today I hustle. Innocently I overtake two "real men" from Alaska. Look over my shoulder now and again on my route up the ice to check whether I'm faster than the others. Building myself up to the approaching summit attempt. Last chance, so it's now or never. Still extremely hard work, but at least I'm finding my way easily, even though the Icefall changes from trip to trip. On the last steep pitch, I encounter Michael Knakkergaard Jørgensen on his way down.

"Where are you heading down from, Michael?" I check out his Lowe fleece jacket, which is covered with sponsor logos. Good idea for my next expedition!

"I overnighted for the first time at Camp III. Anatoli is up there now. I arrived yesterday around noon. Felt great. It was wild, lying there, reading and screaming with laughter at 24,000 feet, utterly alone. And then it froze. Ice cold. I slept like shit and felt queasy this morning, so I just want down."

It's delightfully freeing, chatting and being with Michael. He's honest about mountaineering—no attempt to play the hero or put some value on climbing that it does not have.

"Take care going down. Now it's my turn to sleep up there; we can share horror stories when I return—if our timing works out." So far, Michael has been up acclimatizing on Everest when I'm down resting and vice versa.

Our team's Camp II is located in the most exquisite spot in the Camp II village; unfortunately, for that breathtaking beauty, we have to suffer through a hazardous ascent up the glacier moraine at a time when we basically don't have the energy left to move one foot in front of the other.

Whiteout in the Western Cwm now. The Cwm—a gorge carved out of the mountains by the Khumbu Glacier—is a giant, glacial snowfield, so when the snow and fog come in around noon, everything thickens into one white mass. I'm following the already trodden trail painstakingly, so that I won't fall into one of the innumerable crevasses. To minimize the risk of getting lost and disappearing forever down one of the subterranean ice cave systems, the "road" is marked with bamboo sticks—two sticks marking the visible crevasses, ladders placed across those too wide to jump. I have to be constantly alert—not being able to see a crevasse doesn't mean it's not there. The altitude, length and—when the sun pounds down—the heat and the bright light radiating off the snow, ice and valley walls can make passage through the Cwm torture. Add to that the risk of snow and ice avalanches thundering down from the surrounding mountains.

"Hey!" I greet Martin, who's standing in the middle of the Cwm, pulling on an extra layer of clothes; the Cwm's desertlike heat when the sun is out can quickly turn into an Arctic chill when snow falls. I continue without pausing. Will reach Camp II in one go. The weather can change quickly up here. Actually, we've been fortunate until now, as it's been mostly fair—sunny and not too much snow—so we haven't had any delays because of the avalanche danger that follows heavy snowfall.

Up in the thinner layers of air, where I'm headed, gales have roared almost constantly. At 26,000 feet the subtropical jet stream blows nonstop most of the year. Typically, there's a temporary lull in the stormy weather in May—a few days of clear weather that's called the "weather window." But it can't be counted on. An expedition may spend years training and preparing, ascending and descending the mountain as we're doing now, and then not have the chance to go for the summit because of weather conditions: Nature determines. It's not uncommon that entire expeditions must give up and return home without having accomplished their objective because the weather window never opens. Not summiting doesn't indicate bad mountaineering—one has to look at the entire season, at how other expeditions performed during the same period, under the same conditions.

Becoming harder to find my way now. I'm snailing my way up the last flat bit of snow and ice before the moraine edge, which leads steeply to our camp. Maybe another hour. Suddenly remember other trips, when a tour in the mountains was abruptly transformed from a demanding athletic challenge to a struggle for survival simply because the weather changed.

The boot prints of those passing up and down today have vanished. Have I lost my orientation and walked off the trail, or has drifting snow covered the tracks? I stop, waiting for better visibility. When I spot some tracks, I move ahead, and then look for the next set. I'm soaked with sweat from the earlier heat and now even wetter from melting snow. I consider putting on more clothes, but decide there's no risk of hypothermia.

Now I'm on the crest of the moraine. The visibility is better, and a blue plastic packet on the ice catches my eye. Same size as half of a full-grown man. And that's what it is! The corpse of a dead mountaineer. I can see only the bottom half, dressed in a down suit and plastic boots.

No need for me to go and have a closer look.

I wasn't the first one on the team to come upon one of our predecessors on the mountain. The first time the team overnighted at Camp II, we hiked toward the Lhotse Face the next day to further our acclimatization. I turned around shortly before the rest of the team so that I could catch up with Dale, who had felt like crap during his stay at Camp II and had decided to descend. His problem was clearly altitude sickness: He had a severe headache and was apathetic, withdrawn and unsteady on his feet. When he insisted on descending on his own that morning, I told him I would follow a little later, if not for any other reason than I couldn't, as his teammate, not do it.

Neal, Sandy, Charlotte, Martin and Klev later told me about their "meeting" with a corpse just before they reached Lhotse Face. Plenty of them scattered on Everest: Up to this season, nearly 600 mountaineers have summited Mount Everest, and more than 130 have died on the mountain since it was first attempted in 1921. Those who die are brought down only if they are below a certain altitude and if their transport poses no excessive risk or difficulty. But if a climber dies in or above the Icefall, serious consideration has to be given to the hazards involved in transporting the body back down. If the climber dies high up on the mountain, recovering the body demands an expedition, including the acclimatization process, risking more casualties.

The Sherpas, however, have no dilemma in these situations: They believe it brings misfortune to move the dead.

That day, where the Western Cwm breaks and rises into the Lhotse Face, my fellow team members, one by one, came upon another aspect of preparing to summit the highest mountain in the world—proof that certain risks go with this enterprise, though it took them a few seconds to recognize what they were looking at. Blue trousers, brown boots, one crampon. This was not someone just having a well-deserved snooze. It was the mortal remains of one of our predecessors. The climber must have died on the mountain many years ago, my teammates noted, as the boots were a vintage model.

Sandy at first thought it was Anatoli, pulling their leg. Others hoped the upper part of the truncated corpse was buried under the snow. It wasn't. Under a high blue sky and absolutely perfect conditions for climbing, Martin offered his stomach contents to the mountain gods on the spot.

The corpse lies on the approach to the difficult climb up the icy face of Lhotse, serving as both a guide and a warning about where we might end up. I wonder where the other half is? Perhaps it's been mashed to atoms under the crushing mass of the glacier. Or we may encounter it further up. The South Col is notorious for its inhabitants: Deep-frozen corpses last a long time and move only with the fury of the elements.

The Sherpas would not hear of moving "him." Mother Goddess of the World craves her casualties; she has her rules and those you do not overstep.

Hearing this story has made me pause and consider my own mortality, and now, as I gaze at the blue plastic bag in front of me, like a cairn pointing my way to Camp II, I decide not to seek out this guy's company. I know people die here. I know I, too, risk dying here, and I have no desire to approach the proof.

There will be more plastic bags from here on up. Other expeditions and the environmental clean-up crews, who encounter corpses in their search for used oxygen cylinders and debris, have done what they can to cover the bodies.

O

This is terrible drudgery. The last three quarters of an hour to Camp II is a rising rock scramble, steeper than the rise of the Western Cwm, which itself looks comparatively easy once you pop your head up over the edge of the Icefall. But appearances are deceptive—every time! The Western Cwm is a hard, constantly rising climb. Especially the last bit. Holy hell! Even the high-altitude Sherpas take a break every twenty steps—of course, they're carrying huge packs.

Following each break, my brain starts its mind games: "No problem! I'll just shoot up the remaining 300 feet in one go—full speed ahead." But—impossible! After two swift steps, I break through the hard crust and am up to my hips in heavy snow. All I can do is laboriously plod on, fixed on the tri-colored mess tent ahead, the small tent I share with Sandy and the loving smile on Gyalzen's face—coming straight from his heart. I know Gyalzen, our hard-working Camp II cook, is watching me from up there in his kitchen tent and has warm tea waiting in the big floral-patterned Thermos. He'll be happy to see me, as he's happy to see all of us. That's Gyalzen.

So I continue, striving quietly, calmly, tenaciously to go fifteen paces before I lean over to catch my breath and then struggle back into an upright position to go on again.

On the way to my tent is the New Zealander Rob Hall's camp. Last time I passed, I popped my head inside for a little chat with Ang Dorje, Rob Hall's sirdar for the Sherpa climbing team. I first had the privilege of meeting Ang Dorje in Pakistan in company with Lopsang. The two playmates have now grown into men and are leaders for their respective teams. I highly respect Ang Dorje, and it made my heart glad to hear from the flying chatter that day that he's competent, strong and clearly appreciated by his boss. Rob introduced me to the expedition members and invited me in for a glass of juice. There is one female climber on their team, Yasuko Namba from Japan. She's after her last summit, Mount Everest, in her bid to climb the highest peaks on each of the world's seven continents.

Yasuko seems very modest and pleasant. When we were introduced, we held hands just a slight touch longer than the men and I did. There aren't many women on Everest, and I sense a solidarity among us. Everest has plenty of space for us all.

Rob's team appears strong, with good spirit. Their average age is higher than that of top rock climbers, but high-altitude climbing poses different challenges.

Only 150 feet more. Gyalzen is already standing outside the mess tent, waving. I hear laughter. Strip off my backpack and crampons and seek rest—finally—on a stone bench in the tent. *Enough* for today. I'm tired.

"Can I have ramen noodle soup for lunch, Gyalzen?"

"Of course. No problem!" His smiling face disappears into the kitchen. The first time I asked for this cheap instant soup, Gyalzen seemed slightly puzzled. The Americans have brought sufficient food supplies from the States, and the kitchen staff makes an effort to cook

American-style meals from canned mackerel, flour, pasta and the like. And then I ask for something the Sherpas themselves are having! Same scenario at Base Camp, where Anatoli and I struggle in vain to be served the food the porters and staff are having, such as dahl baat, rice with lentil soup spiced with chilies. We seldom succeed—tastes divine when we do.

Spirits are high here. Those of us who are "still going strong"—Martin, Klev, Sandy, Dale, Pete and I—are preparing for Camp III and our first go at 24,000 feet.

Charlotte suffered so much lung trouble when she was last here that she hiked down to Pheriche in an attempt to recover. Tim had been hit with mild pulmonary edema while participating in the Sherpa rescue, so Doctor Ingrid ordered him down, too. I hope he and Charlotte enjoy the pleasures of the lowlands together. Neal and Scott are expected up here tomorrow. Neal needed rest after the rescue effort and Scott, I believe, had some phone calls to make. But not to Edmund Hillary this time. The Internet discussion with Hillary—where Sandy and Scott fielded questions via her NBC satellite phone—is over and done with.

O

Pass the day giggling and tittering, eating, sleeping, drinking lots of fluids and mentally preparing for the Lhotse Face. Anatoli and I joke about the South Col. And we talk about reality up higher.

"What kind of gloves do you use for the summit bid, Anatoli?"

I'm curious about his experiences because his equipment is reduced to a minimum. He's climbed all the way up here using the same sneakers and ski poles he was using when we met him in Gorak Shep. (Turns out the sneakers are no ordinary running shoes, but shot-putting shoes with spikes, a gift from a friend on the Russian Olympics team.) I'm going to use waterproof over-gloves with different types of inner gloves: silk, fleece, wool mittens.

"What kind of love do I use, you ask?" Anatoli replies, a roguish twinkle in his eyes.

So much for my serious inquiry.

"I need *your* love for the summit. To keep warm in South Col, so I do not end up like the butterfly I gave you."

He's teasing me, and we agree to carry out an experiment in the South Col.

"We will meet and be together at South Col and investigate what happens to the body. I believe one of us will die." Anatoli discusses the potential outcome with the other men.

I'm convinced I've just entered into the wisest brash date I've ever made.

The tents must be fastened more securely to the ground. Last night the storm got so severe that the mess tent blew down and the Sherpas fought a true battle just to keep our smaller tents within sight of our camp area. So while my roommate, Sandy, gives her daily report by walkie-talkie to Scott to transmit from Base Camp to the world, I start improving the stone hedges around our tent. Hard, slow work, but good exercise. A gale hits the camp during the night, but I'm confident our tent won't take off, even though I have to draw myself back from the valley of dreams a couple of times and go out into the freezing night to tighten the guy ropes and scrape off the snow. This is beginning to feel like the mountains I'm acquainted with.

Camp II to Camp III

APRIL 27, 1996

I'm taking my time this morning, before setting off to scale the Lhotse Face for the first time. I prefer enjoying the splendid nature up here in solitude and not having to adapt my pace to anyone but myself and the day's mood and shape.

Naturally, I start with ramen noodle soup. No porridge and greasy chapatis for me, thank you.

Slow morning. Sleeping high on the mountain drastically reduces my will and capacity to perform. Dale, Klev, Martin and Sandy started out an hour and a half ago, but I have the whole day to reach Camp III and typically I'm faster than the others. Except for Klev, that is. We're a good fit as far as tempo and the way we are on the mountain.

O

Martin and Sandy stand adjusting harnesses, ice axes and the like on the last flat ice field before the actual ice climbing begins. The IMAX expedition is assembled for filming, and it's time-consuming getting their entire crew up the ropes. Their commands to wait, stand still and climb down again, so that David can film his climbers, are delaying the ascent. Okay with me, I guess—gives me an excuse to take a break at least.

The very first pitch up the Lhotse Face is regular ice climbing, with the aid of fixed ropes. But it's no straightforward task at this altitude. We are actually queuing up to ascend higher up the wall. Creates a false sense of security being in a group like this.

We're taking breaks, chatting, but one entire rope is secured with only one or two ice screws or a two-foot snow stake. Some of the protection and ropes have been "recycled" from previous years' expeditions. Old ropes and ice screws used for several seasons on Everest are not optimal. But they are there . . .

Today, members of three or four expeditions are heading for a night at Camp III, so up to fifteen persons—plus a load of heavy film equipment—are on one rope attached to one or two ice screws. Though Lhotse is not a vertical climb, the ice wall is steep enough that every climber is clipped onto the rope with a jumar and security carabiner at all times.

So, no matter how tempting it is to be caught up in the group stream, when I spot David's film team hanging from the rope, silhouetted against the sharp light, I choose to wait. Climbing at nearly 23,000 feet is the hardest climbing I've ever been exposed to in the mountains.

I peek upwards and spot the Taiwanese. One of the expedition participants is always exquisitely kind to me, giving me fruit toffees when we meet on the ropes—the only way we can communicate, since we don't speak each other's language. Quite exceptionally he is ahead of me today, moving so slowly, however, that I'm concerned he may have fallen ill—until I start climbing the pitch of ice where I first observed him and realize why his pace was so slow. So is mine! It's torture climbing up this blue ice. Hours pass. With no protection, a fall here would probably set a record for the fastest slide down 2,500 feet of ice. Just imagine!

Coming up on Sandy and David and his team. Once again a welcome chance for rest.

"Oh, Lene, I don't feel well. I think I'm about to throw up."

"Do you want to go up or down, Sandy? I'll climb down with you if you feel that sick."

The solution—we climb on together, with Sandy setting the pace and the breaks. Not necessarily a bad solution for me: The less I overexert now, the less time it will take for my body to recover. Steve "The Plankman" catches up with us, white-faced, doubled over and gasping.

At high altitudes, even the most well-trained and acclimatized climbers have difficulty performing, both physically and mentally. The higher you climb, the more difficult it becomes to function. The reduced atmospheric pressure means less oxygen per breath, and, as a result, less oxygen transferred to the red blood cells. The body responds to this deprivation in several ways, including breathing harder. The heart also beats faster and harder. The body has to work harder just to keep up with the increased breathing.

Hours later, I will myself the last 300, 150 and, finally, the last few feet to our camp, which is so far only a five-person tent on a six- to ten-foot-wide sloping ice shelf. A fixed rope goes up to the tent opening and then on to the other expeditions' tents. One misstep here and you're history. On Everest, a classic way to end your days on the planet would be to leave your tent to answer nature's call in the darkness of the night without bothering to put on your crampons or, just this once, not clipping onto the security ropes—one slip, and that's it.

The view here is incredible! But I'm totally wasted and just want to lie down. Demands steely resolve just to arrange my sleeping bag, strip off the outer layer of clothes and melt water to drink. Takes hours. I have to scramble across Dale, whose massive body is right behind the

entrance. At the far end, Martin's making himself at home. Bit of an
experiment to share a tent with Martin: This is the first time we'll be
this close for this long.

Martin's an odd duck. His view of the world keeps him at a distance
from anything or anyone that might complicate his life. Simultaneously
he's got a cynical clear-sightedness and is totally free from romantic
illusions. He's not afraid of giving his opinion, but neither does he
put it on display—that would stir up too much commotion. He pos-
sesses a twisted sense of humor that makes me squirm with laughter.
I respect him because he doesn't pretend to be anyone other than who
he is. No mercy or heroics here, and that I can relate to. Martin reminds me a little of Grumpy in *Snow White and the Seven Dwarfs*, and
I simply can't resist teasing him and pushing him a bit, so I make him
melt water for the rest of "his" team. Doing something altruistic may
not be Martin's first impulse. But that's okay!

On the mountain Martin's a tough climber. Sometimes swift, sometimes slower, but he's tenacious. At Base Camp he wears the most
delightful sailor's cap—white, with folded-up sides. With that on top
of his skull, he looks like anything but a member of a climbing expedition. More fitting in a bar on Majorca. He knows Anatoli from the
1994 Makalu commercial expedition, and it's Anatoli's presence on
Scott's Sagarmatha Environmental Expedition '96 that made Martin
sign on at the last minute.

Anatoli is up at the South Col with Sherpas from some of the other
teams fixing ropes for the rest of Everest's aspiring summiters. Anatoli
has been at Camp II or higher for several days now and must be weakened, so inwardly I'm hoping he's coming "home" to us tonight. I
must protect my investment, so that we can keep our scientific
appointment at the South Col!

"What's your acclimatization plan, Martin—are you heading for the Yellow Band* tomorrow, spending an extra night here or what?"

"I've planned to use oxygen, so I'll sleep here tonight, descend to Camp II tomorrow and then go down. I'm getting fed up being here. I thought Everest would be more of a picnic, but this is damned harsh, and I just want to get it over with and get on with life."

Dale is lying half-dead in what for the rest of us is a very inconvenient place, so he's not revealing anything, but that's the norm for "Cruiser"—the introvert, the quiet giant, who goes his own way.

I'm worried about how best to prepare myself for a summit bid as part of a team that will be climbing with supplementary oxygen when I'm not planning on using it. Doesn't fit together. I have to climb at least to the Yellow Band tomorrow if I'm to have any chance of acclimatizing during this round. According to our schedule, there won't be time for another trip before the summit bid. It's been a terrible grind just reaching 24,000 feet, but now I'm only 5,028 feet short of standing on the summit. Holy fucking smoke!

Martin is coughing, pukes out the back entrance of our tent, but pretends nothing is wrong. Sandy is standing outside. She's been visiting David Breashears, whose camp lies a few feet behind ours. Actually, our tent is on his camp's carved-out platform, so we may have to move to find space for our second tent. No trespassing on other expeditions' sites is the unwritten law of the mountains. The question remains, though, where would we move to? Sites are not exactly an abundant item on the sloping Lhotse Face. Rob Hall has his camp around the next glacier hillock, but the mere thought of having to

---

* The Yellow Band is a distinctive geological layer of limestone visible to climbers as they ascend Lhotse Face to the South Col.

stagger one step further, having spent the entire day reaching this spot, is simply too much.

There's room for Sandy in this tent, but she wants sleeping bags and food from the expedition rations so that she and Steve can spend the night in another tent, one of Henry Todd's I assume. Apparently Martin has had enough.

"Sandy, there's room and a sleeping bag for you in here, but we can't provide for Steve."

The problem seems to be that "the Plankman" has come up to Camp III without anticipating what it demands to spend the night here. He's apparently taking it for granted that someone else will shelter and feed him. That kind of assumption seems totally insane at this altitude, but is probably just a sign of his young age.

The situation's turned Martin sour, but the rest of us are actually relieved. It's so liberating to have a Martin, someone who speaks frankly, so that I, for example, don't have to do it. But Martin just expresses what I'm thinking.

The high-altitude Sherpas are coming down from the South Col, laughing, and I pop my head out and inquire about Anatoli. "He's coming; he's not so fast today." Suits them perfectly. I guess Anatoli, for once, is showing signs of the effect of altitude. He's pushing himself to the utmost, but is presumably experienced enough to know what he's doing.

"Hey Martin, let's melt more snow, so all the water bottles and Thermoses are filled for the night."

I, myself, have great difficulty gulping down anything whatsoever, but know I have to. I force Dale to drink some water. He's no good at altitude. Absolutely useless.

Anatoli arrives and is granted the space in the middle, between Martin and myself. So this is what it's like to be a herring in a barrel with a dented bottom!

"How does it look up there, Toli?"

"The route is okay. Not too much snow until the Yellow Band. There's a pretty steep traverse, and I used some old rope to fix that section. Found a spot with some lee at the South Col—a corpse lies near our campsite, but we will be more secure there than where the other expeditions plan to put their camps." Anatoli knows what he's talking about. The winds through the South Col are so fierce that they blow everything to pieces. Our tent camp won't be put up until the minute we arrive, otherwise there wouldn't be anything left to spend the night in.

Gone with the wind—and plenty of it. We can hear and feel it here when the wind increases up in the Col—our gas cooker, dangling from its strap, swings back and forth.

"Drink, Dale."

"Do you want something to drink, Anatoli?"

I am assigned the responsibility of finding the Swiss Miss cocoa mix in our food storage sacks, an overwhelming task at 24,000 feet. A glimpse of packs of macaroni and cheese turns my stomach. Swiss Miss and instant soup are all I can handle right now.

I coax fluid down Anatoli's throat. He's splendid at taking care of himself, but the mother instinct in me wants him to drink more. He's bossing me a bit. His mood swings when he's under the influence of altitude—he becomes exceedingly stoic, but nothing I can't put up with. Anatoli is very human. He, too, pays the price for his partiality for thin air.

The gale increases. Anatoli asks into space: "Who am I?" And I know he's watching me and my behavior: Is she strong enough for Everest?

Our walkie-talkie isn't working, so we aren't able to report to Base Camp and Camp II between six and seven this evening as agreed upon. But it's no news that the batteries are dead. Wonder if we'll sleep tonight? Or will we spend the next hours in this torpid state, which, actually, is the least unpleasant state up here.

APRIL 28, 1996
Night passes, and the storm rages on. Early morning arrives, still storming. Later—no letup.

If the gale doesn't subside just a bit before noon, my chances of climbing to the Yellow Band are nil and my plan to summit without oxygen severely compromised.

The wind keeps blowing. And Dale is bad off.

"Drink, Dale. And you must get your blood pumping."

"Go to hell. Leave me alone. I'm fine. I just have to rest a little."

Well, *I* feel like shit. I dreaded this. After a hard day of climbing at altitude, nausea and headache sneak up on me slowly, but inevitably. I try to gulp down Swiss Miss. But I'm not capable of conning either myself or the altitude—hanging over the lifeless Dale, I spew my co-coa up and out of the tent.

I need to go up higher to acclimatize for the summit bid, but the weather, the time and my body say *down!* Playing with the thought of staying up here—just twenty-four more hours—and then climbing on. But I know that every hour above 24,000 feet will only further weaken me.

I think Dale is having a serious attack of altitude sickness and must go down to survive. Cerebral edema is my guess, but it doesn't actually matter what it is. There is only one cure, and that is to get him to a lower altitude!

I hear voices outside, which turn out to belong to Scott and Neal, just up from Camp II. They report that the wind isn't as bad further down. There doesn't seem to be anything left but to let go of my resolve to climb higher. Nature determines, and the accumulated information and a reality check signal *down*.

Dale needs close attention, so Scott decides to ferry him down with Anatoli. I will follow in their slipstream, ready to take over in the Western Cwm. But first Dale must have his climbing harness on. He has lost it completely: can't put on the harness, can't stand without being supported. His brain is on standby, and Scott and Anatoli have to make sure Dale is clipped into the ropes as Neal and I struggle to get him dressed.

Base Camp

APRIL 30, 1996
At Camp II, after having escorted Dale from the bottom of the Lhotse

Face, I learned over the walkie-talkie that the Danish support trek-kers Allan Svensson and Jørgen Pedersen would be at Base Camp when I got down. Ugh! I need to vegetate—not entertain. Anatoli and I spent all day yesterday getting Dale down through the Icefall. No Ingrid at Base Camp. She's still with Ngawang, our acutely ill climb-ing Sherpa. It took several days before he could be evacuated from Base Camp by helicopter. Ingrid watched over him day and night, had him in the Gamow bag, feeding him oxygen. At Pheriche, he suf-fered cardiac arrest at the high-altitude clinic and is now hospitalized in Kathmandu, still unconscious and probably brain-damaged.*

Luckily, we've got visiting trekkers at our mess tent, one of whom turns out to be a doctor. I inquire if he would mind having a look at Dale, who's lying apathetically in his tent.

"Dale, there is an American doctor in camp who would like to talk to you."

"Go away. I'm not talking to any doctor. Leave me alone, Lene."

The doctor looks at me, nods and says: "Definitely altitude sick, typi-cal reaction."

He tests Dale, measures out the correct dose of medicine to treat seri-ous cerebral edema and instructs several Sherpas and team members in how best to help Dale. I need to withdraw from the caring role. We are friends, and I see how difficult it is for him to handle my witness-ing his "weakness." I'm also thinking about Terry and Dale's two sons sending greetings over the Internet via Sandy's secretary. It's crazy that he has exposed himself again to the risk of permanent brain dam-age and the consequences that would have on his family. How is a

---

*Ngawang Topche Sherpa died about a month later.

spouse supposed to be able to cope with that?

It is awkward and profoundly unpleasant to watch a big, strong guy like Dale be reduced to a vegetable—a huge, inarticulate, non-responding lump. His reactions up at Camp III correspond alarmingly with the symptoms of high altitude cerebral edema.*

The Danish trekkers—my so-called supporters—turn out to be the answer to my unspoken prayers. Allan and Jørgen are the sweetest, funniest, most rewarding company I could imagine having. Their irony and banter make me howl with laughter. I swear they razz each other like an old married couple, though they've known each other just a short while. But that's another story.

MAY 1, 1996
I'm angry, disappointed, furious. I cry—but only when I'm finally alone. Just spoke with Scott about the tight schedule and the fact that I need one more time on the mountain before my final summit bid to acclimatize sufficiently enough to climb without supplementary oxygen.

Scott has backed my plan to summit without O_2 100 percent, partly because he understands my ambition and drive and partly because it would be good publicity for Mountain Madness if a woman on its team summited Everest without using supplementary oxygen. Scott thrives on giving people what they want, but now he has changed his mind. He can't have me crawling around alone on the mountain, he says, and if I truly want it that much, I can just get up very early tomorrow morning and climb with the Sherpas to South Col. He also

---

*A person who develops HACE becomes severely impaired: Unable to control his muscles, he can't stand or get into a tent or sleeping bag, can't get dressed. Mental dysfunction ranges from confusion and poor judgment to hallucinations, psychotic behavior and coma.

mentions that I didn't make fast enough time getting up to Camp III.

That set me off!

First of all, I'm not willing to let go of my summit attempt without O_2. I haven't had a fair chance yet. Though Camp III was a rough trial, my body can adjust more with time, and the season is just beginning. Second, I can't help feeling that it's unfair of Scott to suddenly press me into an oxygen-based summit bid so that he can stick to his expedition schedule. He should have thought that through before he agreed that I could participate on terms different from those of the rest of the team.

It's ridiculous that he's evaluating me based on other people's judgments. And whose? He definitely hasn't seen me on the mountain in the last few days. Slow! I know he's mistaken and hasn't looked into the matter from all sides. Why didn't he talk with me before judging?

"Do you know why it took time on the Lhotse Face?" I ask. "For one, because I was keeping an eye on Sandy, but I suppose she hasn't conveyed that to you, has she? If I were the leader on this expedition—where people are right to expect some value for the money they've paid—and I had three guides, I would make sure that every time the team was on the mountain, there'd be one guide situated in front, one in the middle and one to sweep the stragglers."

I've just come down from six days at high altitude and need to rest and recuperate before going back on the mountain. If I followed Scott's proposal and went with the Sherpas tomorrow and then came down to get prepared for his group summit bid, I wouldn't stand a chance of getting anywhere near the summit. A completely out of the blue, unrealistic idea. If he seriously believes I ought to be capable of accomplishing something no one else would be able to, then he's more out of touch with reality than I sometimes fear. His suggestions don't square with the knowledge he ought to possess from his own experiences in the mountains.

On top of it all, he ends with, "I'm proud of you. You're doing extremely well."

I explode: "Fuck you, Scott! You distribute your 'You're doing great' to all and everyone whether they're actually doing well or not. I don't need your 'You're doing great.' I can benefit from support like that if it's well founded and coming from a person I truly respect, but I'm not so sure you belong to that category."

Because Scott is the "captain" and, therefore, has the last word, I'll tolerate his terms, but I'm angry, and anger makes me hard as steel and determined. It also numbs me. I've worked toward this for so long, trusting Scott's good intentions, that when his actions belie his words, I become indifferent. That isn't what I want. I feel humiliated because, in a sense, I'm getting "punished" for helping my teammates. Now I have to stop being helpful because I want to summit that mountain!

I feel uncomfortably numb and couldn't care less. Alone and crying.

Anatoli must have heard what went on, because I hear his voice outside my tiny tent: "Lene, may I come in?"

"Take it easy," he says. "I have a plan for you. Use oxygen, and climb with the others. When I've finished climbing Lhotse, we can meet in the South Col and you climb one more time, without oxygen. I will climb with you."

Need to be alone to think. To cry. I feel let down by Scott, who's forgotten his wholehearted: "We're gonna climb this big hill together, no O$_2$." But it was nice, if naïve, to trust the goodwill of humankind, to pretend it can be trusted. As an adult I do know that basically I am alone and can only trust myself 100 percent. I also know that this flood of tears is not just about Everest and Scott but past letdowns as well.

At dinner I go to Anatoli, take his head between my hands and plant a huge kiss on the forehead of the Russian Man. "Thank you, Anatoli!"

"What's that about?" Scott inquires.

But my soul has closed itself to his questions. I don't know what will happen, but I'm grateful for Anatoli's backing, though it's probably meant more as comfort and a wish that I just climb the mountain than a realistic plan.

MAY 2, 1996

On top of my showdown with Scott, my health is suffering. Camp III gave me a high-altitude cough—first time I've suffered severely. I'm gulping down cough syrup, sucking on cough drops and coughing my lungs out, but improving. Got Scott to climb ice with the Danish trekkers today as was promised in the support trek sales brochure. Michael Jørgensen stayed for lunch. Incredibly snug! We discussed the possibility of joining up and climbing without oxygen. Michael has landed in a similar trap to mine on Henry Todd's team. But he's got some secret plan going, so for now he can't commit himself. Kim Sejberg was hit by falling ice on his way through the Icefall; knocked unconscious, he fell into a crevasse and broke four ribs. Thank God, he didn't suffer more serious injuries! But for him, no Everest attempt this season.

Lopsang is sick—coughing and vomiting—but keeps going up the mountain. Charlotte and Tim are back from their trip to the lowlands. Looks as if they've had a fine time together.

Dale must come to all meals, so at least three times a day he has to activate himself and get his system working. He's clearly still affected by cerebral edema. When one of us asks him to pass the salt or tea, he doesn't seem to register it at first; then he comes to a bit and makes an effort to recognize what he's been asked to do. He's calling home almost every day. I feel for Terry—how must it be for her to communicate with Dale when, under the best circumstances, he comes across like a debilitated seven-year-old? The American support trekker, Jim, does a fine job trying to make Dale feel like a human being, but when he's behaving like a kid, it's difficult.

I pray that I'm wrong, but I'm afraid that both Scott and Dale are counting on Dale's going back up the mountain. Surely this can't be more than wishful thinking, because cerebral edema can result in quick death or permanent brain damage. The medical literature says that some people seem to be predisposed to this suffering. Dale! It happens every time he goes to altitude. When you've suffered from cerebral edema once, going up again is not advisable, even if your condition improved by descending. And Dale's hasn't.

MAY 3, 1996

Feel well this dawn. Wondering whether to remain in Base Camp to rest before our summit bid. Martin has gone down to Pheriche, at 14,000 feet, to rest, and Anatoli to Ama Dablam Garden Lodge at 12,400 feet.

Henry Todd invited me for dinner tonight. Yak curry—sounds sublime! Gonna be fun meeting Michael's climbing buddies.

O

An exquisite, stimulating evening at Todd's camp. His expedition is composed of people from every corner of the globe with vastly different levels of experience. But—no doubt, our team is stronger!

MAY 4, 1996
Phoned my parents in Jylland. They're taking off for Crete for two weeks. Perfect timing.

At lunch, Scott announces: "No one plans to climb Everest without oxygen."

So much for him! I say nothing. I'm mad, upset, resigned and through with him. End of story. Now I don't even want to climb Everest; I'd just like to disappear. What a jerk!

MAY 5, 1996
The climb begins tomorrow. I'm not motivated anymore, but will do it anyway, of course—the line of least resistance. Keeping my distance from Scott. Thinking about my sponsors, article for *Ekstra Bladet* and so on.

O

Am okay, even beginning to feel like climbing again. Feeling rowdy and intend to act accordingly. Article for *Ekstra Bladet* complete and okay!

"Hey, is there anybody around here to invite me for a cup of coffee?"

Someone is scrambling over the rock piles outside. It's Torben, a friend from home who threatened to show up here on his travels in the Far East. Actually, I've been hearing reports of him from trekkers who've stopped by for coffee: "A *huge* guy is on his way. He weighs at least 220 pounds!" According to that description, it had to be Torben. I'd given up hope that he would arrive before we left for the summit. Assumed he'd had trouble coping with the altitude and been forced to retreat. But on the contrary! Torben looks and seems to be in better shape than I've ever seen him. He's radiating energy now that he's left Copenhagen.

"How perfect you've arrived. The last couple of days I've been praying for positive input from the outside world, and here you are. God is great. What an unexpected gift." I know Torben understands.

We chat, huddled up in my tiny tent, exchanging experiences. Then we arrange for Torben to remain at Base Camp while I'm on the mountain. How privileged to have a friend to see me off and to greet me on my (I hope) return. I need that.

I am all set to scale the highest mountain in the world—as ready as I can possibly get at this altitude under these conditions. The advantage of oxygen is that my brain will suffer less damage. I'm capable of laughing again and even say to Scott: "I bet I'm gonna end up grateful for your shit!"

MAY 6, 1996

At dawn, Torben sees me off. At the entrance to the Icefall he says: "Lene, you have fought hard for this climb. Take care of yourself now. You deserve to summit. Spend your energy making your dream come true, and let the others take care of themselves. You are here to climb that mountain!"

Torben's words make sense. I know they are well considered and rooted in the mutual experiences we have of helping people to help themselves.

Then he removes the leather string with the polar bear claw from Greenland that's strung around his neck and ties it around mine:

"Go get that mountain, and come down safe!"

Part IV

The Summit Bid

Base Camp to Camp II

MAY 6, 1996

There's a special atmosphere among our team this early Monday morning—a heady cocktail of festiveness and seriousness. It's now that counts. It must be like this being in the Olympics, when years of training have to be transformed into results in a few days. Except for Anatoli, who'll follow later, we're all here—Martin, Tim, Neal, Scott, Charlotte, myself, Dale, Tim, Sandy, Pete and Klev—in itself, a huge achievement. But I have made it clear that I don't think Dale should be on the mountain again, and that I will not function as his "nanny." I don't think it's a responsible decision—not for the expedition and especially not for Dale, even though he insists on going.

Later I'm informed that Dale, Tim and Charlotte have been given clear guidelines by Scott: If they don't make the trip to Camp II problem-and symptom-free, the climb will be over for them. Tim and Charlotte fell out of the acclimatizing rounds because of troubles from pulmonary edema, but as they are climbing with oxygen, the summit bid is worth a try.

I'm in top form. After the latest acclimatizing ascent and the nights at Camp II and III, the pounds just fell off me. Food for thought! I've come to appreciate having that extra body weight to lose from; body mass becomes critical at a pretty fast pace up here. I'm still coughing, but it's not a handicap yet. The propolis lozenges I've been taking seem to ease the irritation, so I hand a box to a young Sherpa who's on Everest for the first time. He's coughing his way up the Icefall, eager to make a good impression so he can rise from kitchen Sherpa to climbing Sherpa. He's strong, but evidently weakened by his coughing attacks.

I overtake Martin. Fast day for me. Splendid, because I'm heading for the summit. Catch up to Scott and Neal for a while. Scott and I giggle over our row, hug spontaneously and are friends again.

"You're doing good; you're fast," Scott says, and this time I accept his judgment.

"I'm looking forward to getting this expedition over with so I can begin to relax and clear my brain," Scott confides.

Yeah, that's what I hope will happen, but, looking back, Scott's said that before and has yet to turn down new offers so that he'd have more time for himself and for his family. I've become so freaking skeptical with age and experience and have learned to heed what people do, not what they say.

If all goes well, this is our last climb up through the Icefall. We've been fortunate that no harm has come our way so far in this deadly labyrinth of crevasses and stories-high towers of ice. We hardly dare express our hopes, for who knows what's ahead? We won't be safe until we have descended the Icefall for the last time, and right now that lies in the distant future.

Scott and Neal are apparently on some important mission, for they hurry on through to the Western Cwm. I join up with my gentlemen friends, Pete and Klev and, on top of the Icefall, we wait a while to see how Dale is getting on. We passed him further down and he gave us the "thumbs up," but now he's nowhere to be seen, and we decide to proceed.

Pete is truly something. Klev and I are among the fastest and strongest participants on the team, yet Pete, "the grand old man," keeps a pace that would kill most and has overtaken everyone within sight. So, doggedly, without pausing, our trio gains on what at first look like black dots traveling the Western Cwm. When we see Scott and Neal gearing up as they leave Camp I, Pete puts it in fifth gear.

When Klev can catch his breath, he tells stories from other trips where Pete beat everyone to the "goal line." I'm thoroughly impressed and, as always, take tremendous pleasure being in their company. Pete obviously has no problems walking and talking simultaneously. He talks about Alaska, about a dog-sled tour his daughter recently undertook with her children—that's the same daughter who lost all her toes to frostbite after a ski trip into the wilderness. What a father to have!

I ask Klev how he reconciles his participation in our Everest expedition with his obviously clear perception of his responsibilities to his family.

"If what I undertake enriches my wife's and my marriage, then we both consider it for the good. And when I talk to Pete and his wife, I learn from them how to make a respectful partnership last a lifetime. Also, once my kids are old enough, I hope to show them all this; that is, if they want to see it. My wife has the same freedom that I do to follow what she considers important and right, in order to change and grow as a person. Look at Pete—he's lived an adventurous life, is still young at heart and, because he's made wise decisions in the mountains, he's still alive."

As for Pete, I couldn't have ascended faster through the Western Cwm than I had in his slipstream, and just before the final push up to Camp II, we catch up with and overtake Rob Hall and one of his clients. Rob certainly isn't slow, but no one can beat Pete's pace at the moment. Klev grins and reveals that Pete simply cannot stand seeing somebody in front of him.

O

Scott and Neal have just arrived at Camp II and are timing us as we come in to camp. I pretend I don't notice, even though I'm content with my pace. During the afternoon, our team gathers in the mess tent and hears some bad news from Martin, who found Dale in the emergency tent we left standing at Camp I.

"Dale's in the tent, claiming he's snow-blind, because he can't see with his right eye. He's vomiting, but claims he just has to rest and then he'll be okay. He wants to spend the night there and then climb up to join the rest of us."

Sandy and Charlotte share their observations too, and I exclaim, hard-nosed: "That man is deathly ill. He must go back down, and that can't happen fast enough! He's a hazard to himself and to the rest of the expedition, too. I've already spent a lot of time on Dale because he can't adjust to altitude, and it's got to come to an end. He shouldn't even be where he is now!"

Other possibilities are discussed: His condition might improve during the night; perhaps it's not that bad . . . I'm far from being a doctor, but if Dale has visual disturbances—and I don't buy for a minute that they're caused by snow blindness—then the accumulation of fluid in the brain has in all probability begun affecting the optic nerves. So I'm not hesitant to say: "If Dale is not escorted down immediately, he risks dying during the night. He totally lost it last time, hasn't recovered and this sounds truly serious."

At long last, Scott makes the decision: "He's going down. I'll talk to Base Camp and have somebody meet me at the Icefall."

"Scott, why don't you ask a Sherpa to help him all the way down?" I ask. "You've already been down with him once on this expedition; now you need to conserve your strength instead of rushing up and down the Western Cwm."

I think it's a bad idea for both Scott and Neal to hurry down and then back up again at this hour, but Scott responds, "Dale is my friend. As expedition leader, I want to be the one to tell him that his Everest trip is over."

Scott and Neal set off for Camp I, and I breathe a sigh of relief. Whether Dale is more or less altitude sick is, frankly, not important to me. What is important is that he get down to Base Camp and stay down there! Charlotte and Tim can reply positively to Doctor Ingrid's health quiz via walkie-talkie, so they stay. Pete has decided that the trip ends here for him. He hasn't been able to sleep without using bottled oxygen at any point, and the reports from the different doctors who've examined him apparently have been such that he has yielded to his common sense. I profoundly respect his choice. He has contributed so much to enriching this expedition. I hug him and express my gratitude for his leadership up through the Western Cwm.

Can it be that the old fox is embarrassed?

Anatoli arrives. He's the strongest of all of us, but has ended up in a weird position in relation to Scott and Neal. It's as if they have bonded like a couple of school kids and are keeping Anatoli out of their club.

Camp II

MAY 7, 1996
Spend the day trying out the oxygen masks and regulators, and packing. I add the Nikon FM2 camera, for summit photos, to my down

suit and woolen underwear. Stock Reeload, a concentrated gel-like energy booster. It tastes like shit, and its consistency makes me gag (in case the altitude or overexertion doesn't take care of that side of business), but the tiny foil packages are a convenient way of taking in nourishment and fuel in a rush, especially when you don't have any urge to eat real food anyway.

Now that I'm forced to use bottled oxygen, I might as well do it properly. "Be prepared!" as the Boy Scouts say. I had listened carefully to Henry Todd's instructions for using the oxygen mask back at Base Camp so that I would be able to assist others and myself in case of an emergency. He attempted to persuade me to take a couple of breaths that day. "Come on, compromise yourself," he teased. But no, I was going to summit Everest without O_2, so for me to take a couple of sucks during the exercise would have been cheating.

I had asked him, "According to your experience, Henry, what is the weakest link in this contraption?"

"The front piece, where the ventilation takes place. It normally ices up with condensation from respiration, so you have to be vigilant about breaking off the ice to get the necessary circulation. And the cold may cause the meter to freeze up, in which case you won't be able to tell how much oxygen is left in the canister."

Klev, Martin and I unscrew the rubber hoses on the two types of oxygen canisters, test flow rates, check for leaks and try to figure out how many hours of hard climbing there are in the small bottle and how many in the heavy one. Pretty complicated to come up with those calculations up here. We calculate three bottles of oxygen for the round trip from the South Col to the summit and back down. Approximately twelve to eighteen hours, depending on what flow rate you crank it up to. There are additional bottles for Camp III and the ascent from

Camp III to the South Col (Camp IV), and then more oxygen for emergency situations. We're experimenting, well assisted by our climbing Sherpas, who know the apparatus better than we do, and by the indispensable, ever-smiling Gyalzen, who most profoundly wishes the best for us. We're all closer now than during our previous overnight stays, probably because we've realized this could be the last time we're together. Though none of us speak of the hazards, we're all contemplating tomorrow and the days and nights that follow.

"Do you feel like going for the summit, Gyalzen?" I pose the question because I believe some Sherpas must consider us incredibly thoughtless and arrogant to imagine we should be allowed to disturb the home of the Gods.

"Yes, that is my highest wish. Now I've been up here for nearly a month, and next time I'm on Everest, I would like to be on the summit team."

"Hmmm!"

We're listening to the "weather" up at the South Col. And it's there! The winds rage, fizz and whistle as if express trains were roaring through the camp. No weather window so far. Scott and Rob confer. They've decided that our two expeditions will start out at the same hour, follow similar time schedules and support each other fixing the topmost ropes, which are not yet in place, as we will be the first teams on the summit this year. One expedition has turned around from the South Col, beaten and battered into retreat by the never-ceasing storm. And the Swede Göran Kropp, who biked all the way from Sweden and aims to climb solo, had to turn around just below the South Summit because of an incoming gale. But he's patient and knows what's required, so he's now in Base Camp, resting, recuperating, eating and waiting.

According to our plan, we're supposed to depart tomorrow, May 8, at six o'clock in the morning, but the way it's storming now, it seems very unlikely. Yet, another twenty-four hours at this altitude will only drain our strength. But that's better than descending all the way to Base Camp, only to start climbing up all over again. So we're hoping.

Camp II to Camp III

MAY 8, 1996

At 5:00 A.M. Scott reports to us that he and Rob have agreed to wait for a couple of hours to see if the wind tapers off. At 6:00 A.M. departure is announced, and our two teams meet at the end of the Western Cwm.

O

We have a ball going up the Lhotse Face. It's nice to get to talk a bit more to some of the other climbers, to get a helping hand from Andy Harris, a guide for Hall's team, and also a New Zealander. It feels safe to move in a crowd, even though it's not.

Arrive at Camp III in early afternoon and indulge in the natural panorama outside our tent camp. It's breathtaking, and the weather gods are treating us with extravagant kindness today. To begin with, it's clear as far as the eye can see, and then clouds come tumbling up from down under, so we are constantly, sublimely, entertained. Since we were here last, two more tents have been put up, so our camp now consists of three. I choose the same tent as last time and once again join company with Martin and Anatoli. Tim, Charlotte and Klev, who all sleep on oxygen, are sharing the second tent, and Scott, Sandy and Neal occupy the third, along with Sandy's satellite telephone. Sandy's latest brainstorm is to have a Sherpa carry the telephone equipment up to the South Col so that she can call NBC from up there. So this evening we can follow Sandy's, Scott's and Neal's official, as well as private, conversations.

Anatoli looks as though he can't grasp what he's witnessing taking place here at 24,000 feet. His favorite American phrase—"Simply unbelievable!"—which he often uses in an ironic way, suits his facial expression tonight. I'm almost embarrassed. But it's Sandy's and Scott's business, so I say nothing.

Now that the summit is so close, I won't think ahead, but simply focus on the present, the now that is. With such a reduced oxygen supply to the brain, it's actually not that hard to just exist and not speculate about more than where the pee bottle is for the night or whether Scott gets his down suit. I find Dale's. We must remember to send it down with a Sherpa load.

Time passes with no profound speculations, not even Anatoli's "Who am I?" I'm on my way to the summit of the highest mountain on planet Earth. I'll do what it takes to get there. That's all that exists right now.

Anatoli and I make ourselves comfortable enjoying our food and drink and our ritual ragging on each other. To celebrate this day I've dragged a bag of freeze-dried Nasi Goreng up here, and the Thai dish becomes rather popular as both gentlemen can actually stuff down a bit of it. A portion normally slightly insufficient for two starving mountaineers seems to stretch at 24,000 feet until three altitude-affected, appetite-deprived people can't finish the lot and can't get rid of the leftovers in any of the other tents either. But we ate! And Anatoli's skepticism when he stirred the pot and inquired what kind of experiment I was planning for them was disproved.

Now we are all well and content in this mini-universe. Even Martin shows his almost-sensitive side, but I don't remark on it—he might turn sullen again! Charlotte and I have been teasing him. She and Martin know each other from the States, and we two are trying to convince him that he'll find himself a sweet wife when he returns home. We are pretty convinced that Everest will evaporate the haze on the landing strip of his emotional life, for even though Martin puts quite a grand effort into being disliked, he's a fine guy, and we do truly care about our team's "Grump."

It's storming. We're concentrating on melting snow and drinking and drinking. Again I'm commanded to search for Swiss Miss in our food bags, which I do grumbling out loud, but secretly smiling, just to please the boys.

Anatoli's hands have swollen up again. I've observed that this happens every time he's up high, but he pretends not to notice.

No turning back now: to the summit and safe return. I'm on the train, with no intentions of getting off. I will not think of the risks. I've decided to use oxygen, starting tomorrow. If I can't be the third woman in the world—after Alison Hargreaves and Lydia Bradey—to summit Mount Everest without supplemental oxygen, I plan to preserve as many brain cells as possible.

Anatoli will be the only non-Sherpa on our team going for the summit without bottled oxygen. Anatoli has had to use oxygen only once, when a Russian expedition leader ordered him to either use it or leave the team. That story helped me in my hours of turmoil. I've had to swallow my pride, too, resign myself to getting the best out of this experience and then learning from it.

Anatoli climbs without oxygen because he claims it's the safest way: "To work at altitude without taking oxygen demands experience because the body doesn't want to react normally and the muscles don't function. I have that experience. Oxygen is safe as long as it flows, but if anything goes wrong and one runs out of oxygen, the body isn't acclimated to cope without it and one risks dropping on the spot."

I must be content with gaining experience above 26,000 feet—using oxygen. Scott has decided to climb with O_2, but not until the South Col.

I'm heading into the unknown—into the "death zone." How will I perform? I put a brake on speculation. During the night I have a dream:

> I'm climbing as one in a crowd of many. I start out late, and though it's tough, I overtake most, climbing upwards. On a ridge I see several persons silhouetted against the sky. Some of them are black.

Camp III to Camp IV

MAY 9, 1996

Starting this morning, there will be no more breaks, no more rest days. From now on, it's exclusively my physical strength as well as my psychological stamina and genetic makeup that will get me to the summit—*if* Mother Goddess is positively attuned to us. I have trained year after year to foster the skills necessary to cope with the enormous pressure I'll be exposing myself to. I trained for climbing high—for the summit.

I do not doubt I can make it. Don't question, either, that the oxygen will be helpful. How can I be this certain? I believe that refusing to doubt one's abilities determines whether one makes it up or succumbs on the way. There's the danger, though, that that same feeling of absolute certainty ends up getting people killed, because one neglects humbleness. But I don't care. I'm going for the summit of Mount Everest!

We have enough oxygen for six hours of climbing per person between Camp III and Camp IV at the South Col, so Klev, Martin and I start from Camp III using oxygen. We are considered the strongest on our team and fast enough to reach the South Col within the six hours. Charlotte and Tim are slower and must wait until they reach the Yellow Band before they can don the bliss of the oxygen mask.

I'm excited. Finally I'm soaring toward heights I've never before attempted, putting my foot on terrain I've studied meticulously in books and in photographs to glean its secret paths. Finally I'll be facing it, be in it, become part of it. I'm proud of myself, proud to have conquered my fear of heights, proud to have a network that makes it possible for me to be here today, proud of having raised the necessary sponsor money, proud to have broken through my own inertia and introversion. I have transformed myself enough to be here today. I am proud of being Lene Gammelgaard, the first Danish woman attempting to scale the highest mountain in the world.

I am proud that I have the courage.

The route runs up the Lhotse Face on fixed ropes. Rob's team and ours form a row of pearls up the ropes toward the Yellow Band. I do my best to keep a proper distance between myself and the next climber, waiting, clipped in with either carabiner or jumar below a solid-looking snow stake or ice screw, whenever I find there are too many on the rope above me. Incredible the way one's margin of tolerance expands: Hardly any of these ropes or protection would make me feel comfortable on a climb in the Alps, but now I couldn't care less. I want the summit.

We're starting early in the morning to pass through the most exposed passages before the sun rises. As soon as the temperature changes significantly, the mountain wakes up and becomes a living entity: The structure of ice and snow crystals alters, creating avalanches, snow melts and rock slides, and pieces of rock loosen and come careening down the face. I prefer that they not come down on me!

Having my face covered with an oxygen mask is not as bad as I anticipated—though we look like a swarm of grasshoppers from outer space—and the oxygen is improving my performance. The dream from last night breaks into my consciousness as I overtake big, strong grasshopper males, one after the other. Know few by name, but gradually identify who's inside the down suits.

The Yellow Band rock formation runs across from Everest over the Lhotse Face, and—aha!—a yellow band is exactly what it looks like. One of Rob Hall's folks is having trouble on the steep traverse from the main Lhotse ice wall and up the rock-climbing section on the Yellow Band. Anatoli warned us about this place. An abrupt traverse, but it doesn't look too difficult, though I consciously avoid looking down to the bottom of the Western Cwm. Should one of the snow stakes anchoring the fixed rope come loose, I would end up down there, a next-door neighbor to the guy in the blue plastic bag.

What's the matter with Rob's client? Must be a he, judging by the height of the creature, because Yasuko, the sole woman on their team, is tiny and weighs less than a hundred pounds. Right in front of me, a down suit stumbles and falls. Anxiety attack or altitude sickness? After approximately half an hour, Rob's client ascends onto the rock, supported by Rob, and the rest of us can step onto the traverse. The delay sends my imagination in the wrong direction: If a strong guy like that is having that much trouble scaling the mixed bit, then it has to be difficult—too difficult for me? Ancient inferiority complexes are hard to overcome. Or could it be that I—plain and simple—am just a better climber or perform better at altitude? An almost taboo thought and realization for a Dane and, particularly, for a Danish woman.

My boots are working out perfectly so far. If you want to keep your fingers and toes at these altitudes, you have to have specially designed equipment. So on my feet I, and most of the others I see, wear Everest One Sports, a layer-on-layer system of two inner boots and an outer shell. I've only worn them for short distances because they are heavy, and weight does make a difference. But I've climbed with them so far on the summit bid, and they're sublime.

Just now I'm staggering about trying to keep my balance on the traverse because one crampon has come off and is dangling in the ankle strap. Keep cool. For God's sake, stay in balance and get that iron back on. Thanks, Tai Chi. At a more secure spot, I investigate and realize that, fortunately, it's only the closing shackle, which must be placed precisely in the groove on the boot. Haven't brought extra crampons on this bid, so I can't lose the pair I have.

Scaled the crux with no effort, and now I'm beginning the rock climbing section up the Yellow Band in crampons. Baking sun—and I'm climbing at 25,000 feet among some of the leading mountaineers of the world. Kind of hard to grasp . . .

Distances are wide and serious here on the globe's tallest peak—hours pass.

O

The weather has deteriorated—wind! What a difference from the summer warmth and "innocence" of just a while ago. Now Everest shows her teeth, and even the smallest gusts remind me of the seriousness of the grasshoppers' mission. A Sherpa team is in front of me; Klev—green down suit, blue backpack—and Rob—red down suit—are about to negotiate another long traverse. I gaze upwards and see Sherpas—a string of little colored beads—ascending an enormous wall that looks as if it goes on forever. Although I've been working for hours without end and am exhausted, there's still a long way ahead. The South Col must be hiding itself in a hollow up behind the massive wall. I don't recall having read any descriptions of this part of the route. The huge rock massif of layered slatelike flakes is unsafe footing and slippery because of the falling snow. But I trust my feet and am confident on mixed climbs. If you're used to friction rock-climbing shoes, which fit the foot very tightly and allow you to feel the rock through the soles, it's an odd feeling to move up rock faces wearing huge boots with crampons attached, but having done it enough, I know my foot will stick where I place it.

Martin—dark-green, one-piece down suit—overtakes me on top of the rock massif. It's storming big time, and I try to follow the Sherpa in front of me so I'll be certain to find the route around the edge of the slate heap.

The gusts are now so fierce I'm thrown off my feet; I have to cling to the rock to avoid being blown off and down the Nepalese side of the mountain. I understand the wind's power—it blew Alison Hargreaves off the flanks of K2. The Sherpa in front of me turns out to be Old Ngawang, Lopsang's father. We call him Old Ngawang to distinguish him from the other Ngawangs on the expedition. Sherpas are named after the day of the week on which they are born, so the same seven names occur again and again. We grin at each other through the storm. We're on the road—having a ball.

○

Aha! So, this is the South Col. A living inferno. Gale-force winds battle us as we struggle to pitch our tents. Spent oxygen bottles and tent remnants decorate the stark, rock-strewn ground, a monument to those who've been here previously. To me, the trash does not deface the landscape, but rather it recounts a tale of men's and women's destinies, like the kitchen middens of the Stone Age.

I shoot pictures with my Nikon until the film comes to an end. I know not to remove my gloves and mittens to change the roll—fingers have frozen for less. My oxygen mask dangles from my neck. I need to feel the wind, sense nature up here. I love it. Simply love it.

Mother Goddess of the World, Chomolungma, Sagarmatha, truly you are the grandest mountain, and I tread upon you with the profoundest respect and awe. Your summit is all I desire!

But my brain realizes, thanks to my winter studies, that the air is so "thin" up here that I couldn't breathe fast enough to get all the oxygen my body needs. In the death zone above 26,000 feet, my body, even acclimated, wouldn't be able to withstand this hypoxia for more than five days.

I stroll around—slowly, slowly—in the "world's highest junkyard," wanting nothing changed. I don't wander far, partly because I'm exhausted and it's already 3:00 P.M. Our plan is a few hours' rest and then the summit bid departure at 11:00 P.M., if the wind has died down. I know the camp area is "corpse free," but the South Col isn't. The people who remain up here are part of Mount Everest's history too, but, for the time being, I can't think about that part. Lene Gammelgaard has reached the South Col at 26,000 feet. I'm proud. No matter what, I have come this far.

Before I disappear into the flapping, Russian-made, tri-colored tent, I check our oxygen stock, a pile of orange pressurized canisters dumped between the two Sagarmatha Environmental Expedition tents. We're stripped down to an absolute minimum in tents, stoves, food and personal kits—only what's demanded for survival and summiting. Nothing superfluous, no luxury. And no room for error, because rescue possibilities are next to none once you've climbed into the death zone.

The gale is so fierce, we take to wordless communication. Klev has spent the entire afternoon melting snow for Martin and me. When Anatoli arrives later, our temporary home bulges with the four of us and our gear. I'm dug into my sleeping bag, wearing as many clothes as possible, except for my outer boots. Wearing them would help us preserve body heat, but they're too huge to fit in the bags. So everyone's boots are scattered around or being used as pillows and gradually transforming themselves into ice blocks.

Klev is in super condition and melts snow without pause. The gentleman insists in his calm, dignified manner on continuing with this task, even though it's only fair that we take over. But that's Klev—even at 26,000 feet!

We are conscientious about drinking—it's now or never for tanking up on fluids. The dry air up here and our increased respiration and sweating dehydrate us very quickly. There won't be much opportunity to get anything in—or out, for that matter—in the next twenty-four hours. Food, however, nobody seriously considers.

Ice forms on the inner side of the tent and sprinkles down on us with every gust. The gusts also cause the tent opening to come apart again and again. It's shaped like a windsock—you crawl through it on all fours—to keep as much snowdrift out as possible. Unfortunately, it's a hell of a task to draw it together while wearing gloves. The gale keeps yanking the tent fabric from my hands while I'm struggling to tie it securely. And every time someone needs shelter or delivers a message or a steaming pot of tea, I have to fight with it again. Speaking of messages, Pemba just arrived, reporting, "Lopsang is sick—he's coughing and vomiting. And most of our Sherpas suffer headache."

I wish Scott wasn't taking the risk of being here.

I keep an eye on how my mates are behaving and performing and pray I can trust myself and the year-long programming of my subconscious—to the summit and safe return. Now is the time for it to take over, because it's a universally accepted fact that you think with your ass at this height: You *believe* you're rational, believe you have your shit together and are making the most intelligent decisions, but the only thing you can be absolutely certain of is that you *can't* be sure you actually have your shit together, because your poor brain is oxygen deprived.

Doctor Jim from the high-altitude clinic in Pheriche shared what his team did when they were climbing Everest. They kept radio contact with the expedition leader, who stayed at Base Camp; each time they had to make a demanding decision up high, they discussed it with the expedition leader, who, because he was at a lower altitude, was more capable of thinking straight. I wish that, this time, Scott would "climb" Mount Everest via walkie-talkie. But then again, we haven't had much luck maintaining radio contact!

David Breashears's tiny yellow walkie-talkies remind me of toys, but their reliability is beyond reproach. Our sinister black ones can't be trusted, so above Camp II we've just accepted sporadic radio communication. Suits me fine, as radios might add to a false sense of security. Who would pick me up if I phoned for help from the summit, anyway? There is no rescue service out here, and no helicopter can perform anything but a crash at this altitude.

I check my plastic toothbrush case. Not that I've brought a toothbrush up with me. It's just unnecessary weight to haul up the mountain— and anyway, mine now needs a total rehab when I get home. The case is Ingrid's invention and just one more brick in her well-thought-out groundwork for this expedition. It contains a syringe filled with one injection of the steroid dexamethasone for treatment of acute altitude sickness. One shot of "dex" gives you a boost for six to twelve hours, enough energy to move down the mountain, closer to safety. We've practiced and practiced symptom-recognition and talked about having the courage to inject someone in the butt, through clothes and all.

My kit for tonight's venture consists of the toothbrush case with syringe, four Reeload foil-packs, sunblock, extra snow goggles, an extra battery for my headlamp and extra mittens. I'll also carry two oxygen cylinders in my pack, and a 3/4-liter water container in the inner pocket of my down suit—where it shouldn't freeze solid—so I can gulp down some fluid en route.

My down suit is a two-piece, with an extra wind suit in case of gale-force winds. Mountain Equipment in England recommended this combination instead of a one-piece suit, but I suffer when I have to tread off on behalf of nature—the suit seems to be a shit-flap short. So, it's off with the down jacket and then down to the ankles with the overalls—a tremendously exposed position up here. Actually, life-threatening under certain conditions. Well, next time I'll know. The wind cover is in the pack with the sponsors' flags, various talismans, extra film and the valuable and heavy Nikon camera. *Fuck!* The backpack is too heavy already, and I haven't even added the two oxygen canisters. My crampons and ice axe await me outside, securely fastened to the front guy rope.

Still stormy. I must rest. Wonder if Scott and Rob will decide to proceed if the storm dies out. I hope we'll take off and simultaneously don't want to—not enough of a stable weather pattern so far. I know I'll follow whatever is decided.

Before resting, I check the oxygen cylinders we have in our tent, sorting out the empty ones. Martin has to freight them out through the rear entrance. Must wake Anatoli to get the tool to loosen the nuts on some of the bottles so the valves from the hoses to the oxygen masks can be screwed on. Imagine finding a full bottle in a critical situation and then not having it function because of a too-tight nut.

6:00 P.M.—storm. 7:00 P.M.—storm. Hard to imagine it calming down tonight or staying calm for very long.

Must have dozed off for a while. It's silent. A little gust and again, silence. Now what? Will it last? What time is it?

8:00 P.M.—Scott and Rob confer. Their conclusion runs from tent to tent: "We'll start getting ready for the summit bid at 10:00 P.M. if the weather remains calm. Final departure time at 11:30." That leaves us approximately an hour to doze before the unwieldy, uncomfortable job of getting into our down jackets and boots begins. Can't help but admire Scott's decision. This kind of gambling must be what's gotten him to the summit so many times. I would have chosen a wider margin of safety and waited below for more stable conditions. But I want to summit and have no scruples. Apparently nobody else does either.

The one who doubts—wants not.
The one who wants—doubts not.

Camp IV to the Summit

MAY 9–10, 1996

11:30 P.M. It's pitch-dark here at the South Col, the only sounds coming from people already departing and from my friends handling oxygen bottles, masks and crampons. As usual I am late getting out of the tent. It took me an hour and a half to pull myself together enough to get out of the sleeping bag and into my down suit and outer boots. Even the simplest tasks demand so much of you—on every level.

Outside I am met by a starlit sky and a line of headlamps—Rob Hall's team already a half-hour ahead of us. The first part of our team is leaving camp now, and I hurry as much as I possibly can. This overwhelming intuitive feeling that I simply must stick to my group comes over me. At no point—under any circumstances—must I risk being alone on the high flanks of Everest. After clumsily getting my crampons on, I look around and catch sight of only one figure. Must be Scott. Rushing up to him, laughing, I note that his down suit is dark blue so I can recognize him on the road.

"Hi, Scott! Is it two oxygen bottles from now on?"

"Yes, it is," he laughs back. We exchange "good lucks," and I hug him big time before I half-walk, half-run after the fading line of headlamps. I must stick with my team and not fall behind.

At first I walk an almost level stretch of rock-cinder and snow. The ground is littered with old oxygen canisters, but after five or ten minutes' walk, the human debris thins out and there is only sheer blue ice under my crampons. Steep, broken blue ice, hard as rock. Crevasses all over, difficult to see in the dark. I've caught up with the headlamps and am with my group—Klev, Neal, Sandy, Charlotte, Tim, Martin—but where is Anatoli? There he is. He stays in the vicinity of the rest of us.

A steep ice- and snow-covered slope leads upward. A fall here and you . . . No, don't get scared. Concentrate on one step at a time. Focus on the person in front of you, and follow. Don't think; don't let the old fear take over. Upward, upward. Where the hell do the fixed ropes start? I've gotten used to having a "safety line" in the most hazardous places during the expedition, and now there are none at the most risky pitches. Rob Hall's and our Sherpa teams have been assigned the task of fixing the ropes so that no bottlenecks develop, delaying the ascent and increasing the risks. How stupid! In other mountains I wouldn't have become mentally dependent on fixed ropes, but here I have become unaccustomed to the mental pressure and challenge presented by climbing first on a route. But, it's okay. After all, this is my first time climbing the highest mountain in the world, and it takes a little getting used to.

Finally—a snow stake with an orange rope. Relieved, I clip the carabiner into the line and climb upward across the ice. Upward and upward. Even with oxygen, it's madly exhausting. There are ropes, but since they are secured only every 150 to 250 feet, safety is probably so-so. But what do I expect if I wish to roam in the death zone?

How am I going to get down again after many, many hours of this? How exhausted will I be? Don't think ahead, Lene. Focus on what you are doing now. There's Yasuko, from Rob's team. Our group has caught up with the advance guard. There's Anatoli, he's a little behind—green down suit, no oxygen mask. Lopsang is easily recognizable in his white Sherpa suit, which he wears over his down clothes, and he has a flagpole sticking up out of his backpack. Between coughing fits, he manages to tell us that he and Scott have arranged for a stunt on the summit of Everest, but he'll not reveal any of the details. He's still ill, but nobody does anything about it.

How much time has passed? One hour? Two hours? The group

progresses at a snail's pace up across a wall of mixed climbing. The fixed ropes have come to an end, and I am scared. Scared of falling and scared at the thought of how on earth I'm going to get down again. Now and then I climb in a beginner's style, down on all fours, just to be in close contact with the steep, rocky ground. I do not feel like free climbing at this altitude and in this terrain, but I continue and come a little more to my senses as I move. This is very real and very dangerous, but didn't I, in fact, expect something like this when I set out to climb the highest mountain in the world? If it were only a picnic, Mother Goddess of the Earth would disappoint me. She cannot do that, nor does she.

The best thing about climbing and mountaineering is that they can't be belittled. There's no getting away with a "in reality it's probably not that difficult, it's just overly hyped so that those who do it feel like heroes." The mountains are not like that. They are real, they are dangerous and they are exacting, and they show you precisely what you can and cannot do. Show you who and what you and others are.

Watching a slide show years ago, at the beginning of my climbing career, I actually thought to myself: It's surely not that difficult, it's not that steep, it doesn't require that much training, it doesn't require that much in the way of skills to make it all work out. Because I belittled the climbers' achievements, I didn't need to respect them or, consequently, envy what they did, something that I, at a deeper level, wanted to do myself, but didn't have the network or the guts for.

As I got acquainted with vertical rock walls, winter climbing and the hazardous beauty of glaciers, I found out that, yes, it is that exacting. It is that difficult. It is that dangerous. And I was scared and happy! Here, finally, was something that lived up to its own image. Something that was not idle talk. Something that commanded you fully, completely—and even more than that—if you wanted to join in.

Something in which you got to know your own limitations and learned to accept that there are some things you'll never fully master, but that there is much you can train for, and that experience is the key to greater adventures. The mountains are the real thing, and they treat everybody alike. The same rules apply whether you are American or Russian or Danish. Your survival and your success depend on you, yourself. In a simple and brutal sense.

Upward, upward. The 3,028 vertical feet from the South Col to Everest's summit are estimated to take at least twelve hours, so there is no reason for false hope. Upward, upward, for a long, long time to come.

The mixed climbing comes to an end. My teammates and I are standing, slightly doubtful, on the edge of a wide snow couloir. The risk of avalanches is high here, but we must traverse to get across to the rock on the other side that seems to leap upward to the Southeast Ridge, our first oxygen depot. Suddenly we see Lopsang's white outfit over on the rock, and in the fading darkness, we catch sight of an oxygen bottle acting as a signpost in the middle of the snow field. We begin a slow plod across the steep snow field, or rather we fight through the snow, which is so deep that we sink up to our hips in several places. The traverse requires several gasping-for-breath breaks. Oh God, I have to get down through this again! One avalanche and good-bye.

Onward. Pull yourself together, Lene. The first sunbeams peek out from atop the ridge, and I can see a group of brilliantly colored spots sitting on a rock island in the middle of the snow masses. Are they birds? People? Or hallucinations? The sun is stronger now, no clouds, divinely beautiful. A view down over Nepal and the surrounding mountain ranges—I get scared, don't dare to look around too much. It is simply too vast here, too far down. I'm profoundly conscious of being in the death zone, and switch to "tunnel vision" so as not to get paralyzed by the greatness, the madness, the surrealism of my being here. I am on my way to the top of the world! It's huge, and it's scary. I fully understand how people die up here. There is more to die from than to live on, and the least bit of bad weather could make the death trap slam shut. Here, there is no safety margin.

○

It is probably 5:00 A.M. when our group reaches the Southeast Ridge in bright sunshine. Those brightly colored spots that played a trick on my oxygen-starved brain turn out to have been people. Sherpas and climbers in our small community exchange smiles and look up toward the ridge leading to the summit. I turn my head and gaze with awe down the side of Mount Everest we have just scaled, thinking of the biblical tale of Lot's wife, who looked back at the city of Sodom and was turned into a pillar of salt. I look out over the edge of this narrow ridge, almost two miles above the Tibetan Plateau. Mountain ranges as far as my vision reaches, sun and blue sky above. Are we up so high that I'm actually seeing the earth's curve?

Got to pull myself together—shoot some pictures and exchange my one almost-empty oxygen canister for a full one. Thanks to the efforts of our high-altitude Sherpas, there's a supply of full oxygen bottles here and, supposedly, a supply below the South Summit, one more advantage of being a member of such an expensive expedition. And one more reason I wanted to climb Everest without supplementary oxygen. Then I wouldn't have to struggle with the question of whether all this help from the Sherpas is cheating a little. But just now I'm thoroughly pleased with the luxury money can buy.

There's Anatoli. How does he manage without oxygen? Same pace as the rest of us (for once). Says nothing. Yes, he is cold. Looks a bit worn out, too. I have no problems keeping warm—so Henry Todd's advice

to me about using O₂ to conserve body heat is true. I take off the mask
to see what it's like without the oxygen supply—just a bit of preparation, so as not to panic if the oxygen should run out ahead of schedule. I can breathe without the mask, so I drain off the condensation so
it won't freeze up or frostbite my face. I've become accustomed to the
device and no longer give it a second thought—as long as it gets me
to the summit.

Where is the summit? Still not visible? There is a short, sloping stretch
of snowy ridge with overhanging cornices, and then we move upward—mixed climbing as far as I can see. Serious business—at this
moment, I'd prefer that all those who call Everest a hike were right.
But they are not.

Can't help but remember Scott's optimism a year ago: "Everest is easy.
Piece of cake. Just a hike!" How I would have loved to believe him,
but familiar with his enticing and contagious enthusiasm as I am, I
decided to wait and see. And sure enough, Lene Gammelklog (the
Danes use the adjective *gammelklog* to describe a precocious child) was
right: The closer we got to departure, the more I sensed his reality
adjustment. Finally Scott wrote me:

> *We'll have fun in Kathmandu, we'll have fun on the trek, we'll have
> fun at Base Camp, and from then on, it will be one and a half months
> of extremely hard struggling.*

The next stage I'm looking at is tough mountain climbing. It's a good
thing I've improved my relationship with ridges, and this one is more
dignified than most. Tibet on one side, Nepal on the other—and, both,
very far down! To the summit and safe return.

To get from this comparatively safe platform of snow up onto the
ridge itself, you have to balance on a cornice hanging out like a terrace

above the Nepalese side of the mountain and too steep to gain a decent foothold on the Tibetan side. The middle part consists of a cracked glacier edge. Up to you to choose among these three evils. Each choice entails its own risk. I choose the Nepalese side and pray to God the snow stays in place.

It holds, and I continue up the ridge, walking on the Tibetan slope till I catch up with Martin, Sandy, Tim, Charlotte and Klev at a big boulder that marks the last rest stop before the top. I try to drink a sip of water and see that the energy drink in my bottle is almost frozen solid, even though it's been in the special pocket next to my body.

Upward, upward, using exceedingly old fixed ropes left by previous expeditions, ropes used again and again, even by expeditions with the best intentions of putting up their own. At this point, you don't care, as long as there is something—anything—to grab on to. The rock—yellow porous sheets warmed by the sun—can't be trusted, so with Tibet far below, even an old piece of rope provides some feeling of security. I'm careful not to put more weight on the rope than is strictly necessary, though.

Come to a standstill for what feels like hours, almost nodding off hanging from the jumar, until somebody up there gets his or her ass in gear so that the rest of us can get on with it. Time goes by. I am tired. How far is it to the top?

Unfortunately, I'm focusing on the notorious Hillary Step, a steep stretch of climbing near the summit that has beaten many a great climber just before the finish line. Charlotte and I discuss whether that's it ahead. What we are looking at looks difficult and permanent enough to be the Hillary Step, but we know we're just deluding ourselves—there is still a long way to climb before we get to it. Upward, upward.

O

After hours of hard, physical effort, I've fallen into a familiar trance. I'm moving instinctively—not thinking, not feeling, not reflecting—just moving, occasionally checking the bubble in the hose to see if the oxygen is flowing as it should. Carabiner into the fixed rope. Jumar on. Next length of rope. Which rope looks the least aged? I almost don't care. Upward. How will I get down these steep, yellow sheets of rock safely? Onward. A snow ridge. Could that be the summit up there? I can see some rock formations and try to force my brain to remember what the summit looked like in all the photographs I've studied. What did it look like on the video Scott made in 1994? Can't use the images, anyway, for the amount of snow constantly changes the appearance of the mountain. Slowly upward, gasping for breath. My poor lungs: They're working like crazy. Hope they can take it. My breathing has adapted to the environment—more rapid and not very deep.

Pause and then onward. Our team sticks together. And we move at an almost identical pace. Then—STOP! Some down suits are already gathered in a small hollow—five to ten crouching people, sheltered a little from the rising winds and with a view of the Western Cwm a mile and a quarter below. I sit down, kicking my crampons solidly into the snow so as not to slide out of the hollow and down. There is the South Summit, and *there* is the Hillary Step!

It's around 11, or maybe noon. It's cold and I'm tired, so Tim helps me check the oxygen content of my bottle. Damn hard work to take the backpack off up here. You have to untangle yourself from the hose connecting the bottle to the mask, check the gauge and then do the whole thing again in reverse. It's nice to have Tim's help. "Almost empty," he reports. Have to think now. From here to the summit and back again, how many hours? Three to five—probably at high flow rate, for the hardest climbing is ahead of us. I've got to find a full bottle of oxygen among those lying scattered around here. And, of course, it must be one belonging to us. Unthinkable to take from Rob Hall's cache.

Nobody has been on the summit ridge this season, so there are no fixed ropes, only those that have survived from previous summit attempts. The other expeditions at Base Camp supported our two teams climbing first, as it will make it easier on all those coming after us this year if we've fixed new ropes, just as we're using our predecessors' ropes. I look across the cornices toward Tibet and see fixed ropes from previous expeditions hanging in open space, like telephone wires, 30 and 50 feet below me. They emerge from the snow wall in one place and disappear again in another. Wonder if I could grab one of them if I fell . . .

Everything seems to have come to a stop. It's being debated—a little desperately—whose job it is to take the lead fixing the next pitch of ropes and, consequently, who will be the rope fixer on the Hillary Step. Neal thinks it ought to have been done already. Who has rope? Who has snow stakes? Nobody. More feverish gesticulations. Anatoli sets out, followed by Neal and somebody in a blue down suit from Rob's team who suddenly shoots ahead with a rope on his arm. Who is that? He doesn't seem okay. I huddle in a crouching position, freezing in the rising wind. Charlotte, Tim and I agree to stick together. Charlotte is honest: She plain and simple doesn't like this situation.

I watch Anatoli with deep respect. The Russian man climbs deliberately up the Hillary Step, a fly at nearly 28,900 feet above the surface of the sea, his years of experience expressed in his assurance. No panic, no words, no trying to get praise. He does what needs to be done. And does it well! I hold my breath till he is safely up, but know he won't fall. He is too good.

Not many feet of rope to secure us with and no useable old ropes—
they're covered by the winter snowfall and impossible to pull out.
The first stretch on the ridge is an extremely exposed traverse—
spooky—like walking on a tightrope in a strong wind, knowing full
well there is no rescue if you stumble, if the crampons catch your
trouser leg, if the ice axe's grip isn't good enough. I start out—have to
turn back—return to the imaginary security of the hollow, feels so
protected . . .

Must think. Is the summit worth this kind of risk? If I fall, I'm dead. I
can turn back here—others have. The wind has picked up, and I can
see the snow drifting across the summit ridge. There is no security
beyond my own capabilities—do I want to summit that much? Con-
template what it will be like when I return home, what I will feel
every time I see the summit ridge and Hillary Step in my mind and be
forced to face my own defeat. Think of my promises to the sponsors.
Think of the possibilities I will miss if I turn back now—as I have
previously turned back.

I want to get to the top of the highest mountain in the world. I want to
be the first Danish woman to reach the summit of Mount Everest. I
know I have the experience to climb the next pitch, know that it's
only old fears that stop me, know I have the resources in my mind to
break through them. I want to get to the top—whatever the cost—so I
get up and start the traverse on my way to the top of the world.

I'm climbing like a beginner—stiff, unsteady, staggering and, therefore, a real danger to myself. Lopsang sees me. He has never seen me
like this before. He takes my hand, and it helps, even though I know
it's more dangerous than if he hadn't. After barely a few steps, I am
an adult again. The paralysis disappears, and my body moves fluently.

In goes the ice axe with the shaft pointing down; I hold on to the blade and have better support than without it. Lousy axe for climbing. What was Scott thinking of when he recommended it—has he forgotten what it's like up here? I would have felt much better with a long-handled classical axe. Well, next time I have to trust my own experience more. Up across the snow ridge. Every time I take the axe out of the snow, I make a little peephole through which I can see Tibet—there is next to nothing to walk on, but we still do it. I trust myself again and begin to enjoy the madness of being so close to the top on a dangerous stretch of climbing. I can make it. I have what it takes.

Sandy sits down in the snow. Exhausted? She has otherwise done well. There are problems getting quickly past the Hillary Step. It takes Yasuko half an hour, maybe a whole hour. I slip easily up and over, thankful for many years of rock climbing. Was that the notorious Hillary Step? Piece of cake. *Whoopee!* I did it!

Will the summit never come? How far can it be? There's Martin on his way down.

"Congratulations on the top, Martin." I'm happy for him.

Klev follows. The gentleman's dream has come true.

"Congratulations on the summit, Klev." Soon it will be *my* turn.

What's happening? A blue down suit sits cross-legged in the snow. Something is very wrong, but somebody is with him, and Rob Hall, who is a very careful and serious expedition leader, is right up ahead. There is nothing I can do, so I walk on. Pass Lopsang, who is throwing up. I pat him affectionately on the back and smile to thank him for his kind encouragement when I was trying to cross the frightening traverse earlier.

There is the summit! I recognize the metal survey stake from innumerable pictures. I stagger the last few feet.

I made it! I have reached the top of the highest mountain in the world! Satisfaction mixed with fear washes over me. I have to get down again—but how in the world am I going to get my ass down from here . . . The valleys I could see before are now covered with white clouds—but the sky above me is deep blue. There's a wind blowing. It's around 2:30 P.M., I think, or is it 1:30?

I made it, damn it! I have reached the top of the world! I am 29,028 feet above sea level; snow, ice and mountains below me—*everything* is below me—as far as I can see.

Am I euphoric, uplifted, overwhelmed, disappointed? No, I am not disappointed in Mother Goddess of the Earth. I am proud. Quietly, silently, massively content. And then I am tired. Maybe I'll have to climb up here once again just to enjoy the view or have enough strength left to notice whether there is one. It is too much right now. I just want to get down safely. Christ! I am really here! At the top.

We congratulate each other. Anatoli is already gone. First up—first down. I say hi to Rob, who is standing there talking to his collar. Walkie-talkie. Well, yes, some people have these. I thank him for keeping a watchful eye on me down below when I reverted to childhood. Everybody seems happy and satisfied—in fine shape, even if we are tired, of course. Who wouldn't be after what we've been through?

Sponsor photos? I have no energy for anything, but now's the moment I have to pay back what others have given me. Off with the backpack and out with the plastic bag containing the logo flags. Neal agrees to take pictures, and nobody at the summit believes their eyes when I pull the front page of *Ekstra Bladet* out of the bag:

Lene Gammelgaard, First Danish Woman Atop Everest

Too much! I feel people gaping.

Neal took off his outer mittens to press the release of my camera. His fingers are already frostbitten, and he sanely refuses to shoot any more pictures. I've begun to feel pressed myself. I've got to get down from here. And that can't happen fast enough! Flags and camera are thrown into the backpack. Charlotte, Neal, Sandy and Tim have begun the descent, and again I am driven by the compulsion that I must not be alone on this mountain. I have to stick to the group. It is take-off time! Lopsang is unpacking his flag arrangement and waiting for Scott so that they can play their boyish pranks.

There is the man himself—Scott emerges over the ridge above the Hillary Step. Pure joy at being together again.

I hug him."Good to see you, Scott. I made it! I'm tired. Get down safe!"

"Congratulations, Lene! You're the first Danish woman on top of Everest. I'm happy. And so tired. See you down there."

We part, heading in different directions on the top ridge.

Down from the Summit

AFTERNOON, MAY 10, 1996
I hurry to catch up with the others. It looks as if Klev is helping somebody across at the South Summit, or are they taking a break?

Down, down, keep your balance—most of those who perish on Everest do so on their way down. Set your foot precisely, place the ice axe and take just one step. Clip into that bit of rope, and get down the Hillary Step. I made it. I fucking made it! Now I just have to survive the hours to the South Col, then to Camp III . . .

Down, down past the traverse where I had to stop on the way up. Now I hardly recognize it—doesn't seem as steep. Next the oxygen cache. How is my oxygen situation? Almost empty. How many of us are there? How many full or less-empty bottles? I check several bottles in the pile: empty, almost full, full—there's no system any longer. Order has changed to chaos. I exchange my oxygen bottle and calculate that the contents of the new one will hardly be sufficient to reach the South Col, but the further down I get, the safer I will be. So down I go, onto the bad fixed ropes, round the corner, and POW!

Full gale-force winds and snow! *Fuck!* This is serious. The clouds I saw from the top must have been a snowstorm building up further down, and now we're heading right into it. Tim shows the stuff he's made of. Calm and deliberate, he proves himself capable of responding superbly whenever the situation gets truly critical. Charlotte is a lucky woman. I'm on the rope and hurry down after her and Sandy. Tim is after me.

Sandy suddenly sits down and does not want to move. Somebody shouts, "If you don't pull yourself together *right now*, you will die!" and Charlotte unzips her down suit, finds her emergency kit and gives Sandy a shot of dex, just as prescribed, in the buttock through her clothes and the whole caboodle. It helps a bit. We confer and discover that Sandy's oxygen bottle is approaching empty. As I am the strongest among us, she and I exchange oxygen containers, and I hurry on.

I want down, and it is late. I clip into the rope leading down across the yellow sheets of rock. Where there was naked rock five hours ago, there is now a covering of seemingly bottomless snow, like soap flakes. The snow is scary, like quicksand under my feet. Though I can no longer see very far, I know that there's a drop-off to the left, and that climbers have quite literally disappeared in this area without a trace. I hope the fixed ropes can stand the weight of our bodies—we have all clipped in. Neal has taken hold of Sandy. She doesn't seem to be all there, or is she?

I quickly discover it's not possible to glissade on my feet in this snow. It's too dangerous, so I sit down on my ass and slide down Mount Everest. When my speed threatens to get out of hand, I lean against the fixed rope with my whole body and try to brake a little with the carabiner. If the fixed rope snaps, I'm done for. We stagger, fall, crawl, slide, swim our way down the mountain. Our worst nightmare is materializing around us—bad weather! Sheer survival now.

It seems like it's taking forever to get down. Neal is having trouble with Sandy. Charlotte, Tim and I are in fine shape, considering. In the course of a few hours, we get down to the spot on the Southeast Ridge where we took a break at sunrise. Somebody is sitting there—Klev. He's preparing to descend the rock flank leading directly down to camp. In good weather, it would take one and a half to two hours to get back to our tents—who knows how long in these conditions.

NIGHTFALL
It's probably close to 6:00 P.M., so we simply have to be off. The body is almost finished. Exhausted. No food or drink since when? Yesterday afternoon. It feels like an eternity.

Neal is with Sandy. Tim and Charlotte are doing fine, so I hurry up and join Klev. We go directly down the snow flank, where there's a danger of avalanches—even more so now with the snowfall. Slow, exhausting. I start to struggle and discover I'm out of oxygen. *Shit!*

"Stop, Lene. Oxygen! Breathe deeply, and keep breathing. Take some more!"

Evidently, the sudden loss of oxygen made me hyperventilate. Klev can see how blue my face is. Myself, I didn't notice anything.

We work our way down, and Klev insists—despite my protests—on sharing his remaining oxygen with me. For some time he climbs down, and I continue sliding on my ass. My down suit tears, and the down creates its own snowfall. It doesn't matter now—a down suit can be replaced, and I feel safest going down this way. The visibility is getting worse and worse as darkness falls and the snowstorm increases. Sliding on my ass, I at least won't trip over my own legs.

There's a fixed rope, so we are at any rate in a place where people have been before. Who's that in front of us, emerging from the storm? It turns out to be Yasuko Namba on her way down the rope. It gives us hope to see someone else. I am glad she's on her way down. After some time, Klev and I pass her.

It's almost completely dark now. I have a spare headlamp battery in my backpack, but neither of us considers it worthwhile to struggle with changing the battery right now. The advantage of the headlamp is that you can see better within the field of the light beam; the disadvantage is that your eyes adjust to the light and you no longer can see the outlines of the landscape around you. For me, it's a matter of weighing how best to find my way—with or without a light. The light seems to reflect off the snow, turning the whiteout into a snow wall, so for now, it's best without it.

"Klev, I think we should keep to the right at the couloir—don't you see something down there that could be the lights from camp?"

"Yes, let's head for that."

We struggle downward. The whiteout and gale-force gusts make it almost impossible to get our bearings. Every outline of the landscape has been blotted out. Fatigue and lack of oxygen don't help either. Mountain climbers have lost their way up here before because of bad weather. Many simply lose their orientation and walk over the edge of the precipice on the Tibetan or the Nepalese side. The roar of the storm prevents us from hearing any yells from Camp IV, and Klev and I are reluctant to tax our decreasing resources by crying out ourselves.

Cool calm pervades us both. Survival!

LOST ON THE SOUTH COL

"What is that over there to the left?" Klev and I can feel the ground under our crampons becoming less steep, a sign we've probably reached the outskirts of the South Col and are down from the steepest descent. We're trying desperately to find or recognize something that will give us a hint of the camp's location. Why didn't anyone think of fixing ropes all the way down the steepest part? And a rope ought to have been tied to our camp! But it's easy to be wise after the fact, and it doesn't help us now. We stop and talk about the best possible way of finding our way back to camp so that we don't end up as permanent inhabitants of the South Col.

"Quite a bit of light over there. But I think the camp is to the right."

"I totally agree."

But still, we decide to investigate the lights to the left and begin to struggle through the rising storm. Enormously exhausting just to find a foothold and move my boots forward in this lunar landscape.

The lights turn out to be our teammates—Tim, Charlotte, Neal, Sandy, two Sherpas—and two down suits, one of which I think is Yasuko. Klev and I defer to the Sherpas' experience. After all, they've been here before. Looking for known terrain, they poke their ice axes down into the layer of new snow and examine what lies under it—rock or ice.

How long do we all follow the Sherpas—a quarter of an hour? half an hour? longer?—before we realize they are lost? Now they don't seem to have the slightest idea where they are and begin to walk around in a bewildered way and without any apparent plan.

O

It's very dark now, stormy, a blizzard, really. If the Sherpas can't find the way, it means the worst has happened: We are lost.

"Okay, what now? We need to stay together and agree on an action plan so we don't waste energy." I think of a phrase I carry with me— it sounds like a joke, but it helps you stay calm in situations like this: "No, I am not lost; I just don't know where I am right now."

Klev and I are in agreement. We hardly need words to know what the other thinks, and we do what we consider most expedient. I leave it to Klev to talk with Neal. Calmness is the only thing that works in catastrophic situations.

We begin to search the South Col, sticking together. Yasuko is clearly on the verge of losing consciousness, but there is nothing we can do other than try, to the best of our ability, to get her to follow the rest of us. We progress at a snail's pace in the blowing snow. Can't see anything, do anything. A little upward, a little downward. It takes the utmost effort just to stay upright, let alone move our feet. It's a difficult terrain to walk in. Nobody is allowed to sit down or fall behind. We know that equals death up here. The storm, the hope of rescue, the unreality of this living nightmare make us exclaim again and again, "There's light. I can hear voices." But again and again—disappointment.

The Sherpas are no longer with us. Where are they?

The terrain under my feet feels all wrong. Too much rock, too steep and at the wrong angle. Last night, when I started out, I was walking on ice, and there's too little ice here and too few empty oxygen bottles for this to be even in the vicinity of the camp area. I think several of us realize we're headed toward the abyss of Kangshung Face, and we decide on emergency plan No. 2. We have now walked around and around, using survival energy in our search for the camp. We haven't succeeded, and instead of using further energy, our best chance to survive is to find a hollow, a boulder, something—anything—that can give a little bit of shelter against the raging snowstorm, and then huddle together and hope for a break in the weather later tonight. Or, worst case scenario, keep each other warm enough and awake so that we have a chance of surviving the night. At least some of us.

I lie next to Klev, no, half on top of him. Klev has one arm around me. Neal and Tim are on our right. Up against my body, Sandy lies moaning, "I know I am going to die. My face and my hands are freezing off." Charlotte lies next to her, lifeless. She has given up. Some time ago she said, "Just let me be, I just want to die in peace. A little further away in the darkness is the Yasuko bundle and her unknown companion. I don't know anymore where the Sherpas are.

"Keep moving your hands and feet. Say something, shout, keep the guy next to you awake!" Neal, Tim, Klev and I take turns shouting, moving. Klev shakes me. I shake him and kick Sandy every few minutes: "Are you awake? You must not go to sleep. Hold out!" Sandy moans, "I just want to die."

Tim is nothing less than fantastic. He does all the right things in the right way and takes care of everybody in the group. Calm, deliberate, in control in spite of the circumstances. Neal tries to guide, but I sense fear underneath his words.

The gale continues to blow. It's even darker now as most of the headlamp batteries have given out. Everybody's oxygen has run out.

"Charlotte, are you awake?" Tim shouts mercilessly. Charlotte is lifeless.

Snow is starting to pile up on top of Klev and me. Soon we will be just another bump in the landscape. I get halfway up and brush most of it away. Snow crystals begin to penetrate my down suit, collecting in the seams and melting—soaking through my last armor quietly and inevitably. I debate with myself if I have enough strength to take off my backpack. The buckle broke on the summit, so the hip belt is tied around my waist. I'd have to take off my gloves and mittens and work it loose with my bare hands . . . but it might be worth the risk, for at the bottom is my wind suit. That would keep out the gale for some time . . . but I'd also have to get the climbing harness off . . . and crampons . . . I don't have strength for so much, and the risk of losing a glove or . . . too huge . . . so I lie down again.

"Sandy, wake up. You are not going to die."

"My hands," the yellow suit next to my body cries. "They're freezing off."

How tragic. Has Sandy reached the summit she aspired to for so long, just to die or end up maimed?

I fear for Yasuko and her bundle over there. Absolutely no sign of life.

How long have we been lying here?

I know I'm not going to die tonight. I just know it . . . I am not scared. I realize our situation, without fear or panic. My turn has not come yet . . . I am not going to die now . . .

I can still move my toes inside the boots. I guess they are all right—bending them—stretching—bend—stretch—on and on . . . My fingers are cold . . . I move them, beat them against each other when I have the energy for it . . . Bend, stretch . . . Damned gloves. Not good enough for Everest. The outer cover is stiff as a board. Frozen to ice. But it protects against the gale. Try to put the mittens under my armpits to protect my hands against the storm. But too much snow collects—making me still colder . . . Bend, stretch . . . bend, stretch . . .

"Klev, are you awake?" Of course he is.

Kick at Sandy.

"Sandy, check if Charlotte is awake."

Tim works tirelessly. He and Neal try to get Charlotte and Sandy to sit up. Anything, the smallest sign of a will to live rather than apathetic surrender. Yasuko has long since stopped responding. She is blessed, in a way. Is the person sitting next to her dead?

Bend, stretch, bend, stretch . . .

I lie across Klev shaking uncontrollably from the cold. My teeth chatter in my mouth, and the shaking is not of this world . . .

Bend, stretch, bend, stretch . . . make fists of my hands inside my mittens. Move my toes.

How long have we been lying here . . . one hour, two hours?

I don't know how, but through wordless communication, Klev and I collect what is, very likely, our last strength. Somehow we know, without discussing it, that our only chance—and, consequently, the group's only chance—to get out of this situation alive is to perform the impossible right now: to get up and find the camp. Neal has come to the same conclusion, and just then, the weather gods look upon us with mercy. The gale and the snowstorm pause just long enough for a mountain massif to emerge at our right. And I think there is a star. Neal believes he has some direction now.

The trio begins to stagger forward. Klev tries to drag somebody. Yasuko? Charlotte? There's nothing he can do. He has to shake the person off his arm; otherwise he will die here. It takes everything just to keep upright and more than that to move our feet.

"I know where we are, and I know where the camp is," says Klev, and the sense of focus in his voice and the certainty of his movements make me believe in him. Neal is on my other side. He seems to be quite affected by the efforts he has made and the lack of oxygen. He's confused, but struggles to stay in control.

I know I have to stay on my feet, not stumble and disappear. Walk! Now I see Everest to the right and Lhotse? To the left . . .

"Klev, light! Ahead, to the left . . . I'm quite certain."

Camp IV

MAY 11, 1996

Hope . . . stagger along . . . to survive . . . the survival instinct is all there is . . . the will to live.

There's a tent, two . . . I need to pee, so I pee in my down suit. There is nothing I can do about it. I am exhausted.

And there is Anatoli. It was his headlamp we saw.

Neal disappears into his tent. Klev tumbles into ours, falling to the ground like the trunk of a tree.

I look at Anatoli through the storm. He looks at me—knows it is serious—bends down and takes off my crampons.

"Anatoli, the others are out there. They're dying."

"Where?"

"Not far. Walk straight ahead. That way."

I crawl into the tent. Know this is the time when people die. Martin is sleeping. Klev has done everything he could, and now he is out. I am cold, shaking, whimpering like a beaten dog. My body reacts, and my brain takes care of . . . Oxygen! Where's an oxygen bottle with something in it? I take Klev's empty bottle, unscrew the tube and mount it on a full bottle. Manage somehow to attach it to my hero. I can't do any more for him now, he's asleep. Liquids! No snow, only a block of ice in the pot, and I cannot get the gas burner lit.

Shaking and moaning . . . Oxygen for myself. Have to do what I can to help my exhausted body. Prepare a place for Anatoli to sleep when he returns. Where is Scott?

The storm drives right through the tent fabric, leaving a fine dust of snow in the air. I lie in the sleeping bag shaking, shaking with cold fits. My fingers begin to ache. Are they thawing? Am I crying? I moan and cannot do anything about it. The body speaks its own language. Somehow find dry mittens to protect my hands.

"Where are they?" Anatoli is back and angrily demands an answer from me.

"You have to head straight across the rock, not upward across the ice. Straight across the rock. No longer than half an hour."

Then he is gone. Couldn't find them in his first attempt. Hope he does not get lost, too.

I must get the tent opening closed. I must! I try without using my aching fingers. Cannot! I must keep the snow out! I struggle and struggle and finally succeed.

I shake with convulsions and howl . . . the sound of a human animal.

What time is it? 2:00 A.M.? 3:00 A.M.?

Pemba, the only one of our Sherpas still functioning in Camp IV, enters the tent with enough tea to cover the bottom of one of the big pots. I am deeply grateful and touched at the incredible amount of work it must have been for him to boil the water for this cup of tea.

"No more gas," he says.

Am I waking up Klev? The cup of tea Pemba poured for me splashes over my sleeping bag. The shaking fits make it impossible to keep the cup still. But I have to get a little inside of me—how long has it been since I drank anything?

I hear Anatoli coming back with Charlotte. Thank God, then, he has found them—and his way back!

The storm continues. I doze, shake and whimper. The oxygen helps, and I have turned it up to high. Lopsang suddenly crawls halfway through the opening. Even in this ghostlike atmosphere, there is no doubt it is him. The white Sherpa suit! It must be three or four in the morning.

"Where is Scott, Lopsang? And how are you?"

"I'm fine. Scott decided to bivouac up in Camp I. The weather is too bad to come down."

Then Lopsang is gone again. "Camp I" is the name the Sherpas have given our first morning stop on the Southeast Ridge. What can he bivouac in up there? But Scott has been in heavy weather before, so he knows how to survive. Strange decision, but in this kind of weather, not incomprehensible. And Lopsang seems quite calm.

Sleep. Wake up. Anatoli is back. It's starting to get light. I look at Anatoli. He's finished. Empty. Drained. Finished!

We don't need to say anything to each other. I know he has gotten Charlotte, Sandy and Tim "home," half-dragging, half-carrying the two women Tim had stayed behind with. And I think "the Russian

Man" went back to Yasuko and the other one out there and must have been incapable of doing anything for them.*

His nose looks terrible, and his hands are enormously swollen. Anatoli gets into his sleeping bag. I have to zip it up for him with my swollen fingers. Kiss him on the forehead. Anatoli is finished, and he is very quiet—gone deep inside himself.

"Anatoli, Scott is still up there. We have to send some Sherpas for him," I say.

Lopsang crawls into the tent.

"Lopsang, you have to get a couple of Sherpas to go up and get Scott down." I persist.

Now Lopsang tries to rouse Anatoli. "Anatoli, the last thing Scott said to me was: 'Get Anatoli, he is strong, he can get me down.'"

Anatoli is finished. Lopsang is finished, and no Sherpas are capable of climbing up at the moment. From an objective point of view, it's too dangerous. The risk of getting killed is too great. I would probably collapse if I tried any major kind of exertion.

"We have to get somebody up there."

Why the hell did Scott decide to spend the night up there? If he can only keep warm enough to avoid severe injuries! Lopsang seems calm, so nothing serious can have happened. There's nothing we can do until somebody has gotten some rest, and the storm has subsided.

---

*Yasuko Namba perished on the South Col. The other person left behind was Beck Weathers, a client on Rob Hall's tem; he later managed to stagger back to Camp IV, alive but badly frostbitten.

I struggle again to lace up the opening of the tent.

MORNING

"Wake up! Wake up, Lene, we need to get down." Pemba sticks his upper body through the tunnel opening. "Get everybody ready for ten o'clock."

It's still storming. I just feel like lying here. Need to rest, just twenty-four hours more. But my brain knows rest will not help up here, only further weaken me. I am cold and still shaking. Check the oxygen gauge—the bottle is empty. I'm whimpering like an exhausted child. Know we have to get down to survive, but haven't got the faintest idea how I am going to find the strength to move.

Has Scott come down during the night? Maybe he's on his way down now that it's light? We must send up a team with oxygen for him so we can get him down. How far up is he?

"Martin, Klev—wake up! We have to get down. We're off at ten o'clock!"

Wonder if we can get through the storm at all! Thoughts of others who have died from exhaustion, caught at high altitudes in stormy weather, rush through my head. We have to get *down*.

It's 8:00 A.M. I kneel in the sleeping bag trying to melt some water for us. The pot is frozen solid, the lighter won't work and my fingers will not obey me.

I scream—my lower legs are cramping. I struggle to find an oxygen bottle with just a little bit left in it, but the bottles all appear to be empty. Klev has woken up, but can't open his eyes. He's snow-blind.

But still he and Martin start massaging my aching legs.

"Lene, do you have Ingrid's eye ointment nearby? Would you make a patch for my eye?"

Time is dragging by. It is still storming and my hands are useless— *how are we going to get down?* I wonder. We must. I finally find an oxygen bottle with something in it and put on the mask again. My involuntary whimpering stops.

A patch for Klev's eye. But how am I going to get my inside pocket unzipped? That's where the ointment is, in the toothbrush case. Even with the strings I tied to the zipper, my fingers cannot really get a grip on it. It seems to take forever, but finally I manage. Ointment, toilet paper and sports tape. If we were under different circumstances, we would be howling with laughter at Klev's "patch," but right now only the wind is howling. Anatoli is quiet, just lying there.

Lopsang appears. He is still wearing the white Sherpa suit. He is less calm now—less composed.

"We must get somebody up to get Scott. He is ill, very ill. He cannot come down by himself. I had to leave him and Makalu Gau not to die myself. Scott said 'Go down and get Anatoli. Tell him to come and carry me down. He is strong. He can do it.'"

But Anatoli isn't capable of anything just now. The rescues have taken everything out of him.

"Lopsang, get hold of some of the other Sherpas. We have to get up to Scott."

Anatoli is totally out right now, but I know he will stay on the South

Col until he has regained enough strength to climb up to Scott. I just know . . . that's the way he is.

"Klev, Martin—we have to get down!"

None of us want to move. But we must. If we can. Infinitely exhausting to get out of the sleeping bag. Infinitely exhausting to get the down suit on. The others are still wearing theirs, but I had to take mine off. Is it dry now? Doesn't matter. My body clearly shows it's used up, so I have to protect it as much as possible. On with the wind suit. What seems like an eternity goes by. We are so tired.

No news about Scott.

"How far up are they lying, Lopsang?"

"Up there—maybe an hour, maybe two hours from here."

You idiot, Scott. So close to camp and then not coming down. Mountain climbers have survived nights in the open before—but not without losing fingers or toes.

I am used up. There is nothing I can do other than get down alive and try to speak firmly enough to get the Sherpas to climb up again. But basically, I have no right to ask anybody to risk his life for climbers who are too weak for the conditions of Mother Goddess of the Earth. The Sherpas have their own ethics at 8,000 meters, which I neither wish to nor can interfere with. They want to survive—and that is the only right thing to do. I respect their choice. Lopsang will do the right thing.

"Come on, we have to get down."

Out of the tent. Klev will need help to find his way down the mountain.

Camp IV to Camp II

MAY 11, 1996

Pemba takes hold of me and says something I don't quite catch, the words blown away by the storm. Something like "All the Sherpas love you, so I want to help you down." But I hardly know him, this young man who has appointed himself my guardian angel today. Pemba starts walking, pulls at my hand, and I have no choice but to follow him through the storm. Martin is close behind.

From Camp IV to Camp III, this young Sherpa supports me. He takes my carabiner from one rope to the next. My fingers are still useless, so he clips me in and takes me off each rope—quickly and efficiently. I follow him down at a pace I could not have set in my condition without the close protection of this angel of mine. What was it he said up there? Did I hear correctly? The further down the mountain we get, the more the storm weakens. How strange it is to suddenly be able to hear Martin saying something behind me. I wonder how Klev is doing?

The sun is shining.

Pemba is good. Very good. Only makes the most necessary movements. First he secures himself, and then he secures me. I'm not allowed to use my hands. He is steady. Everything he does serves a purpose; nothing is superfluous.

I wear the oxygen mask to do the little I can to prevent my body from collapsing. Outside of Rob Hall's Camp III, people come out to meet us, tears in their eyes.

"Welcome down. How fantastic to see you alive."

People are on their way up to offer any help they can—up there where we came from.

Camp III. I tumble into our tent, Martin after me. Klev, Sandy and the others can't be seen up on the route. Pemba waits for some time, then he's on his way down.

I try to rest, but start to whimper again. Funny. I can't help it. No words exchanged. Nothing to say. Martin and I would like to stay and rest, but at an altitude of 24,000 feet—there is no rest. We have to get down, so we set out together. Martin is quicker than I am, and we part. I am careful to secure myself to the ropes all the time. I know it's at this point that fatigue can mean a careless and possibly fatal mistake. Slowly, slowly I move down across the Lhotse Face, pausing more than I have ever done before.

"Lene, how good to see you. Is there anything we can do for you?"

It's David Breashears and Ed Viesturs on their way up. How strong and normal they look.

"Do you have anything to drink? I am so thirsty. Dehydrated. I can't remember when I last had any fluid."

David squeezes my hand. "We thought you were all dead. Last night twenty-one were reported missing."

So that's why people are so happy to see us.

"How is Sandy?"

"She's on her way down. She must be en route to Camp III. She probably has frostbite, but she is alive."

I drink and drink—cautiously, in small sips, so as not to get sick.

"Rob Hall is lying right below the South Summit with a dead client. His feet are frozen—so when he tries to get up and walk, he falls. But he has radio contact most of the time. They fear Scott is dead. Sherpas are on their way from Camp II with more help," David says.

We part. Ed and David are on their way up to help. They have an oxygen cache at the South Col and are in excellent shape, so they'll be a welcome sight.

Don't think. I'll believe Scott is dead when I hear it directly from someone who's seen him dead. I still silently hope he'll come walking into camp with his usual roguish smile. Both Lopsang and Anatoli are still up there—they haven't given up.

I can see a line of antlike black dots below me, heading for the Lhotse Face along the trail in the Western Cwm. Looking forward to being down there myself. Longing for someone to carry my backpack and more to drink.

Down the last steep stretch of ice. My body does not want to work this hard anymore. Whoops!—one of my outer mittens flies off. Doesn't matter now; it's at the bottom of a deep crevasse, and I don't feel the need to climb down there to get it back.

O

Finally at Camp II. Someone takes my pack, and I take off my crampons, harness and everything else I don't need for safety. A helper hands me a mug of steaming hot tea.

Stride through camp, badly in need of seeing one of the other Danes: Henrik, Bo or Jan. I don't know where Michael is. I need Henrik's professional knowledge to help with my hands. Am told the Danes have set up an emergency hospital in Rob Hall's mess tent.

Congratulations sound around me. Heads emerge from tent openings. A "well done" from a subdued voice. An atmosphere of gloom and pent-up feelings hangs in the air among the brilliantly colored tents.

Henrik, Jan, Bo. They are there, all three of them. Familiar faces from back home. Under these circumstances—almost family. I'm led inside and feel instantly welcome and taken care of. Mal Duff is here, too. He looks forlorn. I think he and Rob are best friends.

Henrik diagnoses minor frostbite, prescribes some medicine and forbids me to use my hands for anything for a long time. "Into the sleeping bag, and drink, drink, drink," he orders. Bo appoints himself Florence Nightingale and promises to come up to my tent and help me. Jan Mathorne jokes and talks.

Henry Todd stands outside. Big bear hug and comforting laughs. "Ah, those fingers are nothing. Mine have looked like that lots of times. In six months they'll be completely healed."

"Are you okay, Henry?"

"Yes, I am quite fine. Michael and the others are at the South Col, but I've told everybody to come down, except for the two strongest ones, who'll stay there and help out."

Photos are taken. And then I am finally home again. Gyalzen. Ramen noodle soup. But where is Scott? Anatoli? Lopsang? The rest of the team is slowly on its way down, being met by helpful Sherpas.

But what about Scott?

Part V

ॐ

After the Storm

Camp II

MAY 12, 1996

Our team is gathered. Somebody must have walked through camp and beaten us up, one after the other, with a baseball bat, judging by the way we look: Swollen eyes. Boxer's nose. Black cheeks and lips. Flesh peeling off. Crying and laughing alternately as reality sets in. And we are still not down: We have to get through the Western Cwm. And down through the Icefall—for the last time. The tension of months is replaced by apprehension of the myriad things that can still go wrong.

Reports from the camps up above repeatedly confirm that Scott is dead. Lopsang is on his way down, and I'm waiting to hear what he has to say before I declare Scott dead to myself.

Lopsang comes down the cliff. We are waiting, the Sherpas are waiting. I go to meet him, and he breaks down in my arms and sobs. The therapist in me diagnoses shock while the friend in me listens to his flood of words. A story he will be telling again and again.

"Scott is dead. My father went up to get him down. My expedition leader is dead. Scott is lying up there in the snow. Lene, he was ill already at the top. He came up to me saying he was so tired, so tired. Scott took a picture of me. I had to put a rope on Scott on the way down. He tripped and fell and would not move. On the snow flank he tried to glissade down toward Tibet. I had to lower myself on a rope to get down to him and get him up again. I have never seen Scott like that before. He just gave up. He said he was going to jump right down into Base Camp. And I dragged him and begged him to keep moving, but on the ridge he just did not want to walk any longer. I could not get him to do it. He took off his oxygen mask—he would not wear it even though there was more oxygen—and he just kept saying, 'Lopsang, I am so ill, so ill. You have to get hold of a helicopter.' I did not know what to do, and he said I should go down and get Anatoli. 'He is strong, Lopsang, he can carry me down. Tell Anatoli to come and get me.' I lost him, Lene, I could not save him. He gave me his camera with all the photos."

Saturday morning, at around ten o'clock, a team of Sherpas had climbed up to try to find Scott, among them Lopsang's father—Ngawang Sya Kya. They found Scott and Makalu Gau, the Taiwanese expedition leader, where Lopsang had dug a platform for them the night before. The weather was still brutal, and Scott was barely breathing and had almost no response at all to the oxygen or hot drinks, whereas Gau was fully conscious. The Sherpas took care of the stronger of the two and had to leave Scott behind.

Saturday afternoon Anatoli climbed up to Scott and found him dead. Anatoli did what he could, under the circumstances, to cover Scott's body and took a few small things of Scott's to bring back to Scott's wife and two children.

O

Ritzau News Agency
May 13, 1996

NINE MOUNTAIN CLIMBERS FEARED DEAD
ON MOUNT EVEREST

Wellington, New Zealand—Nine mountain climbers are feared dead this weekend on Mount Everest in the Himalaya, the highest mountain in the world. A total of 24 mountain climbers from four different expeditions were on descent from the mountain Friday when a violent storm broke, according to reports from foreign news agencies.

The *Ekstra Bladet* writes that thirty-four-year-old Dane Lene Gammelgaard, the first Scandinavian woman to climb the 8,848-metre high Mount Everest, is alive. The leader of the American expedition Gammelgaard is a member of, Scott Fischer, is reported missing and feared dead.

Base Camp

MAY 13, 1996

Finally, Anatoli is down. I breathe a sigh of relief. The Russian man is sitting among us this evening in our mess tent. The rest of us have been thoroughly treated and bandaged by an efficient but weeping Doctor Ingrid.

"Thanks for being alive" and a big heartfelt hug were what she greeted every one of us with as we stumbled into Base Camp. Ngima, Pete Schoening and my friend Torben had met us far into the Icefall with hot drinks and grateful hearts. Sadness, grief and joy flowed, seeing each other again.

We survived. To the summit and safe return.

Out of our team of eleven American and European climbers, only Dale and Pete didn't take part in the summit attempt. Of the nine who went for the summit, all got there. One died on the way down—our expedition leader, Scott Fischer. Scott would have been satisfied with his team.

Now we are sitting together, missing our leader. The mountain kept one of ours, and Anatoli is the last one to have seen him. I have a need to ask, and Anatoli has a need to tell. Anatoli is a changed man. He is worn out and clearly weighed down by Scott's death. I wonder if he feels guilt about not having been able to fulfill his friend's last wish? An impossible burden to carry.

My instincts, intuition and common sense take over: "Drink your tea, Anatoli." Every time he looks away, a teammate fills his cup again. Anatoli is a proud man and difficult for anybody to "take care of." But the strong are also human.

"Anatoli, where is your other down parka?"

"I do not need it."

Sure he does. "Steve, would you fetch Anatoli's down parka?" My hands are bandaged like boxing gloves to protect my fingers against further injury, so I need help myself for every task. But command I still can. When Steve puts his own parka around Anatoli's shoulders, Anatoli wakes up a little, walks to his tent and puts on his big blue down jacket. In the meantime, tea is poured. Then the Russian man puts an end to any hidden hope with his account of how he found Scott dead.

MAY 14, 1996
At the memorial ceremony, Anatoli concludes his speech to the dead—given through tears—with the following words: "Sorry, I came too late, Scott."

I let go, saying, "Thank you for making this possible. I will continue to live in the way we believed life should be lived—'Let's make it happen and have fun!' I will miss you, Scott."

MAY 15–20, 1996

The expedition members begin departing. I stay as long as possible, taking proper leave of Mother Goddess of the Earth who has kept my good friend. I need time to think and grieve. To be among mountain climbers, among the people who share the story. To let my soul heal just a little before I start the journey back to civilization and the hectic times I can expect once I'm back home in Denmark. I need to remain here long enough to say a proper good-bye to Scott, in my own way.

Anatoli will climb Lhotse, fulfilling a plan he and Scott had made in February. He is physically and mentally "out of order." The mountain climber in me knows he has to do it to become whole again. That is just the way it is. Doctor Ingrid does not understand. If she continues to return to the big mountains, she will gradually come to understand. I understand that she does not understand.

I have started taking vitamin pills again. Anatoli asks to have the ration Scott used to get. I gladly carry out the ritual even if it is difficult to get the tablets out of the foil packages and plastic bottles with these bandaged hands.

In three days, Doctor Ingrid becomes skilled at making bandages that don't get torn to pieces during the twenty-four hours between bandage changes. With Velcro on everything these days—sleeping bags, tent openings, clothing—how does a person with gauze boxing gloves for hands keep from looking like a streamer?

Syangboche Airstrip, Above Namche Bazaar

MAY 20, 1996

The rest of the expedition, that is Klev, Neal, Pete, Martin, all the climbing Sherpas and I, wait in the morning fog for the helicopter from

Everest Air to arrive. We're about to embark on the first serious step of our journey home, the trip to Kathmandu—and the press.

The others flew out some days ago—Charlotte from Base Camp because of frostbite on her toes. When we finally got down through the Icefall and she took off her boots, her toes were bloody lumps. Sandy hired a helicopter from Pheriche a few days ago, and Ingrid and Tim joined her.

"There is one boarding pass too many," Ngima says.

"I bet it's for Anatoli. He will probably show up at the very last moment."

Rumors have reached us that Anatoli climbed Lhotse and that Michael Jørgensen turned back just below the summit because of bad weather. They are both alive, and that's what matters.

The helicopter, delayed because of fog, lands finally, and the whole circus starts trying to get the Sagarmatha Environmental Expedition squeezed into the metal body. I wonder what system they use? As the cabin gets full, they unload the sacks in front that have just been loaded from the back! They say there's too much weight for us to get off the ground, after which they weigh the baggage on some enlarged bathroom scale and put it all back in again.

Anatoli, where are you? You promised you were going to fly out with us today.

Five minutes before departure, a purple hat appears at the end of the runway. Anatoli.

Anatoli is in order again. It's clearly reflected in the serene lines of his face. He summited Lhotse, the fourth highest mountain in the world, without using oxygen, right after our ordeal and walked (ran) all night to be here now. He brought his guitar.

Simply unbelievable!

EPILOGUE

"Triumph and Tragedy" the media proclaimed the spring 1996 Everest season. Many people have said to me, "What a shame, that the biggest victory of your life should be connected with so much pain."

I don't see it that way. I knew when I set out to climb Everest that it would have a price. I just didn't know how high a price Mother Goddess of the World would exact to show us humans the consequences of hubris. Natural laws do exist in this universe, and Mount Everest is a mighty, yet simple, example of how we can—or can't—conduct ourselves and not come to harm.

Everest—pure, divine, unmanipulatable, vast, deadly and profoundly rewarding for a short while—just as life can be anywhere. But more so than most places, Everest shows you what you are made of in that brief period that seems a lifetime. It changes us.

Returning to Denmark, I became a celebrity. A gift in several ways, but also limiting for the wild animal I am at heart. The publicity gave me the opportunity to work and work and work—overwork. After two years, I had exhausted myself and ended up severely ill. I hardly believed I would ever recover. But I am a survivor. I had turned myself—consciously—into a workaholic, with the sole purpose of not having to feel, not having to grieve just then. Needing to transform a catastrophe into something better, I continued working along the lines Scott and I had planned.

Now, three years after the expedition, I can no longer escape the grief, the profound loss, of not only Scott but also Lopsang, who died in an avalanche off the Lhotse wall a few short months after our climb. A year later, Anatoli, my ethical and aesthetic anchor in this world, also died in a climbing accident. Three grand personalities and very giving people. It's three too many, and I am marked by fate, yet grateful to have shared some of life's wonders with three extraordinary people who can never be replaced.

The true extent of the loss has become evident over time, as I miss them again and again. No more of nature's adventures planned and carried through with these exquisite soulmates. They are irreplaceable, as big personalities—dream-feeders for the rest of us—always are.

○

Mount Everest taught me a valuable lesson. I will never again expose myself to that amount of objective risk. Never!

Being alive is precious.

Life is so short.

AFTERWORD

On Christmas Day, 1997, Anatoli Boukreev died in an avalanche on the slopes of Annapurna in the Himalaya. Just three weeks before he had been honored with a prestigious mountaineering award from the American Alpine Club for his rescue efforts on our Everest climb.

Anatoli Boukreev—the strong Russian man who became my friend. To me a valuable and highly respected tutor in the deepest sense. Without Anatoli my experience climbing Everest would have been less grand. His presence is greatly missed.

Anatoli was the true mountaineer. Straight and uncorrupted. He never pampered people, but he would risk his life once you were in real trouble. He came from a different culture and was sometimes misunderstood—as tough as the mountains he loved. Anatoli was also a tender man with a philosopher's soul. For those of us who took the time to get to know him, we were rewarded by his fine qualities, which were abundant.

I will let Anatoli speak for himself and explain his philosophy, as I sit back and smile, remembering this genius of the mountains:

> I would like to believe that the roads we choose depend less on economic problems or political battles or the imperfections of our external world, and more on our internal calling, which compels us to go anew into the mountains, to the heights beyond the clouds, making our way to the summits. The sparkling summits and the fathomless sky above our heads, with their grandeur and mysterious beauty, will always draw humanity, which loves all that is beautiful. This was, is and will be the magnetic strength of the mountains, independent of the worldly, trivial vanities and fusses, beyond which, at times, we cannot see the real, the beautiful and the eternal.

GLOSSARY

Bivouac: A night on a mountain—planned or unplanned—without a proper camp. During a bivouac conserving body warmth is crucial to avoid hypothermia and frostbite, so climbers look for a spot out of the wind—in the lee of a rock or in a snow or ice cave.

Bivvy sack: A lightweight waterproof bag used for shelter on a bivouac.

Carabiner: A metal snap-link with a spring-loaded gate to allow insertion of a rope or a runner, used in many climbing maneuvers, including clipping onto fixed ropes.

Chapati: A round flatbread that originated in northern India.

Chorten: A small shrine built of rocks.

Cornice: An often unstable snow or ice lip overhanging the edge of a mountain ridge.

Couloir: A deep chute or gully.

Crampon: A framework of steel spikes that fits over the sole of a climbing boot and is fastened by metal clips or straps. Used for climbing ice and snow.

Crevasse: A crack in the surface of a glacier that can range from narrow to wide and from shallow to hundreds of feet deep. Crevasses are a considerable hazard to climbers when they're hidden by surface snow.

Crux: The most difficult part of a route or section of a climb.

Cwm: A Welsh word (pronounced "koomb") commonly used among mountaineers for a valley ringed by mountains; a cirque.

Diamox: The brand name of acetazolamide, a drug that seems to help in the acclimatization process if used in the early stages and at moderate altitude.

Face: The vertical part of a mountain; wall.

Fixed ropes: Ropes anchored on a mountain to help climbers over difficult passages.

Flowrate: The amount of oxygen flowing from a pressurized oxygen bottle through a tube or hose to the climber.

Glissading: Descending a snow slope by sliding over the surface—either "skiing" down on your boots or sitting on the snow.

Ice axe: An essential climbing tool for snow and ice. The classic ice axe has an armlength shaft, with a spike at one end and a double-ended head at the other consisting of a pick for self-arrest and an adze for digging snow or cutting ice. Axes for ice climbing are shorter and of various specialized design.

Icefall: An unstable, steep part of a glacier where the faster flow produces crevasses and serac build up.

Jumar: A mechanical rope ascender. The metal device clamps onto a climbing rope; it can be pushed up the rope by the climber but it will not slide back down. Used as a safety device on fixed ropes.

Lee: Shelter on the side away from the direction a wind is blowing.

Lodge: A rustic guest house in the mountain regions of Nepal.

Moraine: The banks of huge rocks and debris that settle at the edges and end of a glacier.

No O's: American slang for climbing without supplemental oxygen.

Om mani padme hum: Tibetan Buddhist mantra, translated as "Hail to the jewel in the lotus."

Pitch: The distance between two rope anchors (an aluminum stake hammered into the snow is a type of anchor).

Prayer flags: A long string of Tibetan Buddist prayers printed on pieces of colored fabric. The prayers are believed to rise to the Gods with the wind.

Prusik cords: Thin rope pieces used to tie Prusik knots—sliding friction knots—around climbing rope, which are used like the Jumar.

Puja: A religious ceremony.

Ridge: The crest where two opposing faces of a mountain meet.

Serac: A tower of ice, usually found where a glacier steepens either at the intersection of crevasses or in the area of an icefall.

Sherpa: A mountain tribe of people that migrated around 500 years ago from Tibet to Nepal, settling in the Solo Khumbu region near Everest.

Sirdar: The Sherpa in command on an expedition. Usually an expedition will have a climbing sirdar and a base camp sirdar.

Sling: A loop of rope or woven nylon tape.

Stemming: A climbing technique that uses opposition of arms and legs against two or more surfaces.

Tai Chi: Ancient Chinese martial art.

Thamel: A primarily tourist-centered part of the town center in Kathmandu, the capital of Nepal.

Traverse: To climb more or less horizontally and up across a rock, snow or ice wall rather than straight up it.

Trekking: Rough hiking in the high mountains.

Whiteout: A weather phenomenon where visibility is low or non-existent. Snowfall, snow cover and/or fog combine to obscure landmarks, including the horizon, disorienting climbers.